After Augustine

MATERIAL TEXTS

After Augustine

The Meditative Reader and the Text

Brian Stock

PENN

University of Pennsylvania Press

Philadelphia

10 9 8 7 6 5 4 3 2 1

Published by
University of Pennsylvania Press
Philadelphia, Pennsylvania 19104-4011

Library of Congress Cataloging-in-Publication Data
Stock, Brian.
    After Augustine : the meditative reader and the text / Brian Stock.
    p.   cm. — (Material texts)
Includes bibliographical references and index.
ISBN 0-8122-3602-5 (cloth : alk. paper)
    1. Augustine, Saint, Bishop of Hippo. Confessiones.   2. Augustine,
Saint, Bishop of Hippo—Books and reading.   3. Augustine, Saint,
Bishop of Hippo—Influence.   4. Self-knowledge, Theory of—History.
5. Books and reading—History.   I. Title.   II. Series.
BR65.A62 S745   2001
418′.4′01—dc21   00-068269

for
Goulven Madec

Contents

Introduction   1

1. Reading and Self-Knowledge   8

2. Ethical Values and the Literary Imagination   24

3. Later Ancient Literary Realism   38

4. The Problem of Self-Representation   52

5. Petrarch's Portrait of Augustine   71

6. Two Versions of Utopia   86

7. *Lectio Spiritualis*   101

Notes   115

Index   129

Acknowledgments   131

Introduction

During late antiquity and the Middle Ages, the spiritual exercises that were associated with self-improvement were normally based on extensive periods of reading and meditation. As a consequence, the reshaping of ethical values in these exercises became a part of the subject's inner experience. The present volume is an exploration of this theme.

The figure who appears most frequently in these pages is Augustine of Hippo. This is understandable, since he is the most prolific and influential writer on reading between antiquity and the Renaissance. It is clear to all who have studied Augustine that his writings on the topic have important implications. But he refused to spell these out in detail, perhaps deliberately, and as a result his statements were occasionally quoted by opposing sides in medieval debates involving principles of interpretation, as they were by Berengar and Lanfranc during the eucharistic controversy. It can be argued that medieval and Renaissance thinkers were sometimes too systematic in their presentation of Augustine's views on reading and interpretation. He did not write a treatise on the topic like the *Didascalicon* of his twelfth-century admirer Hugh of St. Victor. His reluctance to synthesize his views on other important themes, such as the sacraments, suggests that he would have been skeptical about any attempt to bring together his statements on reading as a formal theory. Yet, despite the unsystematic nature of his writings on the subject, he remained the point of reference to which later writers invariably returned in their search for the roots of problems concerning reading and interpretation. They were fascinated by his story of how he had sifted through the doctrines of ancient schools of philosophy in his effort to defend the close reading of the Bible as the foundation for the Christian life.

The approach to reading that he developed in his various writings appears principally in his philosophy of language, in his method for interpreting the Bible, and in his personal account of his spiritual education.

His philosophy of language is essentially a way of relating words and things by means of signs. As signs can be spoken or written, the same rules apply in principle to communication through speaking and reading. In this dual approach to the subject, Augustine differs from thinkers in antiquity, for example Aristotle, whose influential *De Interpretatione* is mostly about spoken language. Augustine reflected the ancient concern with speech in his early writings on the subject, *De Dialectica* and *De Magistro*; however, when he turned from philosophy to the study of the Bible in *De Doctrina Christiana*, his interests were focused on written language. The concept of the reader became associated with the interpretation of written signs, and, under the influence of Plotinus, with the modes of contemplation that followed the auditory or visual experience of reading. In the sermons, commentaries, and theological treatises written after his conversion, reading and thinking are closely related activities.

Augustine incorporated his views on reading and interpretation into his portrait of himself in his early years in the *Confessions*. In book 1 he relates how he learned to speak in childhood and to read and write during adolescence. After the teenage misdemeanors of book 2, he reappears in book 3 as a serious reader of ancient philosophy, Manichaean tracts, and (tentatively at least) the Bible. The subsequent period, described in books 4 to 7, marks his transition into the field of interpretation under the guidance of Ambrose, as well as his abandonment of the oral dialogue, with which he experimented at Cassiciacum as late as 386–387, in favor of the written forms of discourse in which philosophy normally appeared in late antiquity. The narrative of these years portrays him as a student who progresses from a youthful infatuation with pagan literature to a mature appreciation of the literal and spiritual senses of scripture. The final chapters of the story take place in books 8 and 9 when he is converted to the religious life by means of a book and experiences a vision of the paradise of the elect, where perfect communication takes place without the need for words. He thus begins the autobiography with one type of speechlessness and concludes it with another.

Augustine took a journey of self-discovery, but in contrast to other ancient authors it was one in which the figure of the philosopher was complemented by that of the reflective reader. In the *Confessions* this contemplative figure engages in the reading of books and the rereading of a life narrative by means of memory. The lessons of philosophy are learned through reading; they are then applied to the reform or, as some would prefer, the rewriting, of a personal life. Augustine left his own readers the transcript of this experience in the narrative books of the *Confessions*, doubtless in order to encourage them to try his method of conversion for themselves. In all likelihood he would not have adopted this solution to the Socratic problem of self-examination had he not been a Christian thinker. The manner in which he united the soul's progress with the theme of the body's passage through historical time was greatly indebted to the Christian doctrine of the incarnation. The individual life thereby became the setting for the reenactment of the biblical drama of alienation and return: a Virgilian retelling of the parable of the prodigal son set against the backdrop of Plotinian neoplatonism.

Augustine's emphasis on the reflective reader likewise offered a new approach to ethical thinking, some aspects of which are discussed in chapter 2. He not only asked his readers to consider philosophy as a way of life, as had other Hellenistic thinkers like Epictetus, Seneca, and Marcus Aurelius: he suggested that the literary or artistic imagination of his readers could play a role in sustaining that way of life. To be sure, by the time he wrote the *Confessions*, between 397 and 401, he had formally rejected pagan literature and ancient philosophy as guides to ethical thinking, unless their doctrines harmonized with the teachings of the Bible. Well before that time, in 386–387, he had adopted a modified version of the Platonic view that literary and artistic creations are misleading. During the same period, he also worked out an essentially negative approach to language as a guide to understanding reality.

Yet, if he maintained these reservations in theory, he had abandoned them in practice by the time he embarked on his autobiography. The narrative books of the *Confessions* are rich in literary inventions, many of them derived from his close reading of classical texts.

The use of literature for ethical instruction by means of the Bible was incorporated into the interpretive program of *De Doctrina Christiana*, which was begun about the same time. Augustine took pains to point out that the Bible persuades its readers through both its doctrines and its eloquence. His early studies in biblical literature in opposition to Manichaeism likewise taught him the value of the Hebraic technique of rejecting external images, as a type of idolatry, while advocating the interior recreation of images in religious narratives in an effort to reshape behavior.

He believed that our moral outlook is conditioned by the literary context in which we situate ethical statements, as well as by the interpretation of those statements within recognizable philosophical genres. He was unsure that any of these genres could reach defensible conclusions through discourse alone. He envisaged the participants in his early dialogues as if they had read some guidelines for behavior before they entered into a conversation on ethical problems. As a result, his students assume that they share some ideas on the issues under discussion before the conversation begins. These opinions may differ, but the participants recognize that they have in common this inner experience; and they are persuaded that this shared knowledge is more certain than the conclusions they can reach by verbal reasoning alone. It is the problematical relationship between this inwardness and the exterior forms of discourse that alters the philosophical context in which ancient ethical questions are asked in Augustine's writings. The first chapter of the *Soliloquies* draws attention to the tenuousness of this connection when Augustine tells his readers that he is not sure whether the voice of Reason with which he enters into discussion is coming from inside or outside his mind.

Medieval authors transformed and occasionally disagreed with the methods of self-analysis employed by Augustine. Some illustrations of the medieval language and literature of the self are found in Chapters 4 and 5. During the Middle Ages there was more autobiographical writing than in antiquity, at least more that has survived, but it is not possible to speak of "autobiography" as a defined literary genre. By contrast, there was a wealth of writings about the self which offered literary alternatives to inherited philosophical and religious statements on the topic as well as to standardized medieval genres such as allegorical treatises on the virtues and vices. The growth in interest in the self was supported by the increasing interest in the linguistic philosophy of intentions. In Augustine the expression of intentions through language was generally subsumed under the problem of the will, whereas in medieval authors after Anselm and Abelard linguistic intentionality emerged as an autonomous topic within the study of forms of speech, largely owing to the influence of Aristotle and Boethius. A branch of this activity was concerned with the analysis of the verbal intentions of God as expressed in biblical writings. A parallel development united the philosophy of linguistic intentionality with the first stages of the early modern problem of individualism.

One of the works of the later medieval period that takes up the question of literary self-definition is Petrarch's *Secretum*, which is the subject of Chapter 5. In this dialogue Franciscus, expressing the views of Petrarch, enters into a discussion with a recreation of the historical Augustine on a number of ethical issues, among them the status of authorship and literary self-representation. Augustinus, presented as a medieval monk, reproves Franciscus for failing to live up to his otherworldly ideals, while Franciscus attempts, not always successfully, to idealize his worldly love for Laura and to justify his authorship of the *Canzoniere*. Augustinus and Franciscus evidently embody different aspects of the literary portrait that Petrarch wished to leave to posterity. The goddess Truth, in whose presence their debate takes place, can be identified with the ideal reader of the *Secretum*, who is enabled through their discussion to examine different ethical positions on the topic of reading and to ask whether they can be reconciled. The *Secretum* ends without a solution acceptable to both parties, but it is clear that Petrarch favors an approach that has less in common with that of his mentor than with the reflective readership of later figures like Montaigne and Pascal.

One of the problems that is touched on in these chapters is the gradual transformation of thinking about the emotions during late antiquity and the Middle Ages. Late ancient thinkers inherited a somewhat simplified version of Hellenistic doctrines on the emotions in which a number of strategies were pursued in the hope of overcoming emotion through reason. In Augustine's early writings reason has both theoretical and practical dimensions; as a consequence it is possible to envisage emotion in some contexts as a complement to reason, for example in the abandonment of carnal desires and their replacement by charity, which leads the indi-

vidual from a material to a spiritual goal. Augustine believed that
the best way to achieve this "conversion" was by means of the meditative reading of the Bible, through which emotions like charity
could become a part of an individual's lived narrative. Contemplative practice thereby helps men and women to attain the objective
of transcending the body that is common to neoplatonic and Christian theology. Late medieval authors added a dimension to this program by viewing writing along with reading as a valid contemplative
exercise and as a record of spiritual experience.

Chapter 6 turns to another aspect of the history of reading in the
early modern period—attitudes toward utopian thinking in Augustine and Thomas More. Unlike Plato, who speaks of the just society
in the *Republic* in largely abstract terms, these two authors prefer to
view the problem of utopia in the context of actual societies. However, they differ on the role of readers and audiences in preparing
the individual for engaging in this type of thinking and in its potential application to everyday life. In Augustine reading is a type of
ascetic exercise that is aimed at preparing the believer for the after-
life. The reader is a type of philosopher who comes to conclusions
concerning the possibility of establishing a utopian state after comparing pagan and Christian texts. The exercise can be compared to
the program for betterment in the *Confessions* in which the personal
memory of one's own past is replaced by the artificial memory of
written records through the study of the Bible.

In More reading is an instrument for the creation of individuals capable of participating in a literate democratic commonwealth.
Reading and writing are vehicles of social as well as personal intellectual progress. The textualized community is envisaged as an end
in itself. Despite these differences, Augustine and More both conclude that a perfect society is unrealizable on earth. Like Plato, they
view utopia as a plan, a design, and, in More at least, a subject for
sustained irony.

The final chapter is an attempt to introduce themes from the history of reading into the traditional framework in which the problem of European cultural identity has been studied by means of
Romance philology and related historical disciplines. The philological approach, which is now about a century and a half old, argues that the unique source of European identity has arisen from
continuity and change in spoken language. An alternative is to suggest that parallel patterns of cultural identity emerged from the

history of language and the history of readership. One of the important developments was the evolution of *lectio divina* into a flexible type of interpretive reading that was known after the thirteenth century as *lectio spiritualis*. This change led to the birth of a number of reader-oriented theories of cultural interpretation that were applicable equally to words and to images. These were widespread during the Renaissance and afterward in thinkers like Montaigne, Pascal, and Vico, who envisaged cultural understanding as a contemplative experience.

Chapter One
Reading and Self-Knowledge

The late ancient and medieval periods inherited a number of techniques for dealing with the classical philosophical problem of self-knowledge. The theme of this chapter is the influence of the culture of reading on the transformation of these techniques.[1]

My major purpose is to address an issue that arises out of the thought of Augustine of Hippo. This is the connection between reading, the search for self-knowledge, and the writing of autobiography. Augustine raised fundamental questions concerning the use of ancient contemplative practices in his treatment of self-knowledge and self-expression. The first part of this chapter takes up these questions in the context of late ancient thought. The second part turns to response during the Middle Ages.

It is desirable, I believe, at the outset, to distance ourselves somewhat from the perspective on self-knowledge that has been created by the contemporary history of autobiography. Since the Romantic period, we have associated the questions of self-knowledge and self-representation with the writing of autobiographies. But the word "autobiography" appears to have been first employed in English by Richard Southey in 1809, and scholarly interest in the subject does not go back much beyond the nineteenth century.

One of the historians responsible for generating this interest was Jacob Burckhardt, who saw the appearance of first-person life histories in Renaissance Italy as a sign of renewed concern with individualism, in contrast to what he believed to be the collectivist mentality of the Middle Ages. Another influential figure who touched on the subject was Max Weber, who initially associated the early modern interest in the individual with the emphasis on self-examination in Protestantism, but later extended his research to other religions in an effort to characterize the features of Western "innerworldly asceticism." Studies of biography and autobiography were deepened by the reflections of Wilhelm Dilthey, especially in his life of Schleiermacher, and by the several volumes of the *Geschichte der Autobiographie* undertaken by his son-in-law, Georg Misch, in 1900. Misch was indebted to Dilthey's conception of *das Leben* as life experienced prior to conceptual knowledge and thought, an idea that found its way into the diverse approaches to self-knowledge in Bergson, Husserl, and Heidegger. Dilthey was preceded in this line of thought by Herder, Novalis, and Nietzsche, who believed that every great philosophy was in some sense the confession of its author. By the turn of the century, it was difficult to carry out an inquiry into self-knowledge without the accompanying notion that autobiographical writing was a privileged means of inquiring into that knowledge. Our time has seen a reaction against this type of thinking that Yves Bonnefoy has aptly called "les illusions du *cogito*."

In general, ancient thinkers did not make a connection between the study of the self, the soul, or self-understanding and the composition of autobiographies. The very idea that the self could be configured adequately in a literary or artistic form was a subject of debate. Medieval students of self-knowledge did not write many autobiographies either, although first-person histories are found more frequently during the Middle Ages than in antiquity. It was only at the end of the medieval period, or, as some would prefer, on the eve of the Renaissance, that a clearly definable autobiographical tradition emerged in authors like Margery Kempe, Petrarch, Christine de Pizan, Benvenuto Cellini, and Jerome Cardano. Among ancient literary works the exception would appear to be Augustine's *Confessions*, which is routinely taken as a point of departure in contemporary histories of autobiography. But the *Confessions* is not merely the bishop of Hippo's self-portrait of his early years; the work also incorporates several ancient literary genres, among them a spiritual exercise, a story of conversion, a treatise on interpretation, and a guide to self-improvement through ascetic practices. In sum, there would appear to be a tradition of thinking on the problem of self-knowledge in ancient and medieval thought, but no single literary genre for dealing with representations of the self, the person, or the individual before the early modern period.

Georg Misch spoke of the lack of ancient autobiographies as a limitation of the Greek spirit. Yet it is not their absence that has to be explained as much as their appearance. The non-autobiographical approach to self-knowledge had an obvious attraction for ancient thinkers as a response to the potential arguments of skeptics. If the self was not represented in the literary or artistic manner the writing of a first-person life-history necessitated, then these types of representation could not be criticized for their inadequacies. Autobiography could remain a problem in the field of self-knowledge rather than pretending to be the solution. The majority of ancient authors preferred to explore the topic of self-description through the concept of *bios*, which referred not to physical or historical life, as it does in the word autobiography, but to a mode of life or a manner of living, in particular to aspects of lifestyle that could be shaped inwardly by the will. In the ancient view, a person's life could be guided by writings, for example, by the *hypomnemata* or *commentarii* that served as memoirs for Seneca and Marcus Aurelius, but writings could not in themselves take the place of lived experience. A form of discourse and a form of life had to make a harmonious whole, a plenitude (*plenitudo*), as Augustine said in *De Beata Vita*, that was not simply a mass of circumstantial detail (*abundantia*). What made a life exemplary by ancient standards was not setting down events in a permanent form but living in an ethically informed manner. It was not clear to ancient thinkers that the writing of an autobiography could advance this program, since the distant origins of autobiography were in rhetoric rather than philosophy. The literary or pictorial presentation of the person could even create illusions about what was essential to the self, as Plotinus observed in his trenchant refusal to have his portrait painted or his life-history set down by his students.

Just as there were different ways of talking about self-knowledge, there were different literary or philosophical genres for representing the self. Rather than offering a single interpretation of the subject, the literary genres of ancient philosophy reflected the conceptions of their authors, schools, and religious groups concerning the moral and ethical expectations of their respective audiences. The question that was implicitly asked in such writings was how a particular configuration of the self would function within the practices of a community, or, alternately, how a behavioral ideal agreed on by the group could be implemented in the life of the individual. The authors of such accounts rarely provide the type of information that would be expected in a modern autobiography, that is, dates, events, places, and extensive descriptions. If we call their writings "autobiographies," we do so on the understanding that the recording of details was less important than the distancing of the senses, the adoption of methods of self-examination, and the rigorous implementation of ethical principles. Within such a plan for living, autobiographical statements frequently related what their authors had learned about themselves, and they reminded readers, who were the potential practitioners of the same mental disciplines, what they did not as yet know about themselves. Self-knowledge was the goal: the literary or artistic representation of the self was a way of indicating the presence or absence of such knowledge in the intended or implied audience.

Augustine renewed the literary and philosophical principles of this tradition. The *Confessions* became the Western model for the literary genre he called the *soliloquium*. This was envisaged as a type of discourse in which a person and his rational spirit entered into debate in the interior of the soul on the preconditions and limitations of self-knowledge. In the *Confessions* the characters in the dialogue were changed, but the philosophical objectives remained the same. There is no doubt about the influence of the *Confessions* on subsequent writings concerned with self-analysis. In his extensive study of the literary history of the *Confessions*, Pierre Courcelle demonstrated that Augustine's masterpiece was widely read in the centuries before Petrarch ceremoniously carried his copy to the top of Mt. Ventoux in 1336. Petrarch thereby helped create the modern interpretation of the work, which consists in viewing it chiefly as an autobiography. Yet it is important to recognize that there are some features of Augustine's story of his early years that make it an exception both to ancient practices in autobiographical writing, to the degree they existed before him, and to medieval works that touch on the life-histories of their authors, such as Petrarch's own autobiographical dialogue, the *Secretum*.

Augustine shared the ancient view that philosophy should be a way of life, but he differed from his predecessors in setting out deliberately to relate the story of his life in detail. He revised the story a number of times, telling it in anecdotal form in his early dialogues and retelling a part of it in his *Retractions* in the form of a doctrinal history of the books he had written. If we study the successive versions of Augustine's life, we do not arrive at a definitive life-history. Instead, we discover that in his understanding of the issues the revision of a way of life as it is lived and the revision of the story that is told about that life have something in common, inasmuch as they are both narratives. This is a literary method in the service of philosophy.

Augustine likewise differed from earlier writers on the theme of self-knowledge in making the investigation of his subjective experience the point of departure for his self-examination. His belief in the value of subjectivity was indirectly supported by the argument of the *cogito*, in which he anticipated Descartes. In response to the skeptical view that our knowledge of ourselves is as problematical as our knowledge of everything else, he asserted that the one thing he knew for sure was the irrefutable fact of his own existence. This proof provided him with a firm foundation for inquiring into other aspects of his self-knowledge. He also reevaluated the role of personal memories in establishing the continuity of this knowledge. The story of the soul's progress or education, which was a theme common to many ancient inquiries into self-knowledge after Plato, thereby became associated with the account of a particular life as it proceeded in historical time through stages of incertitude, self-understanding, and ethical conduct.

Within this interpretation of the notion of *bios*, Augustine differed from earlier philosophers in according an important status to rhetoric. He abandoned the widespread ancient belief that a person engaged in philosophical inquiry should be capable of attaining an ethically satisfactory way of life through the use of reason alone. In place of this view, he adopted the position that reason had to be reinforced by persuasion. Using his personal life-history to support his case, he argued that none of life's fundamental problems can be solved by philosophical reasoning, since the possibility of rational choice only arises when a person is in possession of enough facts to make an objective judgment among potentially different courses of action. In the passage of a life, as it is simultaneously lived and reflected upon, no human is in this happy situation. The beginning and the end of the story are unknown, since they go respectively beyond the individual's memory and experience; and the information he or she possesses is biased, since much of it is based on the subjective evaluation of sense-perceptions.

Augustine was convinced that knowledge acquired through the external senses is transitory, and that it reflects the spatial and temporal situation of the observer. The person who relates his own life, as he did, tells the story within the limits of the knowledge available, not as it would be told by an omniscient author who has all the relevant facts at his disposal. Because this relating appears in a narrative form, Augustine believed that the questions of self-knowledge and self-representation cannot be separated. This was his contribution to the longstanding debate between rhetorical and philosophical approaches to self-knowledge that went back to Isocrates's *Antidosis* and Plato's criticism of rhetoric. Augustine's synthesis of these positions was as important as his pioneering of the literary genre of autobiography, and possibly broader in its influence in the early modern period: it was this approach, rather than the writing of first-person life-histories, that was imitated in the confessional styles of Petrarch, Montaigne, Erasmus, Descartes, and Pascal—authors who were among Augustine's heirs in the search for self-knowledge but who did not write formal autobiographies. In a single masterpiece, Augustine effectively transformed an ancient contemplative practice into a new type of mental exercise that had both literary and spiritual dimensions.

*   *   *

Augustine brought about this change by identifying the reflective self with the reader. The *Confessions* thereby inaugurated the age of the self-conscious reader/thinker in Western literature.

There were of course thinkers before Augustine who read books, but no one before him had inquired so systematically into the role reading might play in support of the life of the mind. In *Confessions*, books 1 to 9, he told the story of the progress of his soul toward God as the evolution of a reader who proceeded from pagan and sectarian views toward the truth of the Bible. In books 10 to 13, he presented an outline of a theory of reading in relation to ancient teachings on grammar, rhetoric, and interpretation. In parallel with his account of reading in the *Confessions*, he outlined a theory of signs that was adapted to the needs of readers of the Bible in *De Doctrina Christiana*. As a result of this theory, his readers, unlike the students of Cicero's *Tusculan Disputations* or Seneca's *Moral Epistles*, were able to connect the relating of a personal life-history to the traditional search for self-knowledge through a consistently argued philosophy of language.

Augustine's achievement took place within a widespread growth of interest in readers and readership in the late ancient period. Reflective reading, including, in the imperial age, extensive reading of earlier philosophical texts, became a major method of inquiry by which individuals attempted to work out ethically informed philosophies of life. The foundations of this type of inquiry in Hellenistic philosophy were ably described by Pierre Hadot in his inaugural lecture at the Collège de France in 1983. Hadot spoke at length of the deep interest of Hellenistic and Roman thinkers in "a form of life" that was "typified by an ideal of wisdom . . . , a fundamentally interior disposition of mind" that emphasized "self-control" and "meditation."[2]

It would be fair to say that Christian thinkers in late antiquity and the Middle Ages shared the search for wisdom with the ancients. They cultivated the interior life. They engaged in a variety of spiritual exercises that emphasized self-control and meditation. Yet, in contrast to their Hellenistic predecessors, much of whose work has vanished, they left behind a large corpus of writings. We possess only a part of this literary heritage, but what we have is substantial enough to lead us to suppose that its survival was not an accident of history: these writings were deliberately created as a literature of meditation, self-governance, and the spiritual life. They differed from their Hellenistic predecessors in their Christian orientation and in their strengthening of the already established connection between meditation, as a spiritual exercise, and reading. As a consequence, the style of thinking about the self that is envisaged in the spiritual literature of this thousand-year period is difficult to separate from the way in which its principal writings are designed to be read.

The connection between reading, devotion, and contemplative practice was not immediately accepted by Christian thinkers. The Lives of the desert fathers are rich in stories about religious men and women who distrusted books and the urbanity of the literary life. Comparable attitudes are found in Eastern spiritual writings: the eighteenth-century collection known as the *Philokalia* records the case of the admirable Arsenius, who never wrote or received letters and even considered speaking to be a sign of vanity. The early Christian suspicion of book-learning is an occasional theme in the ascetic literature of the Latin Middle Ages. However, as a rule, medieval authors agreed with Gregory the Great, who observed that as students of the Bible "we should transform what we read within ourselves, so that the mind, roused by the ears, brings together and puts into practice what we have heard by means of our way of life."[3] The rise of oral reading as a Christian contemplative practice was an important development in Western spirituality. We have as yet only a partial and incomplete history of the techniques in question and their relationship to earlier forms of contemplative thinking.

The new interest in reading in Western spiritual writings can be illustrated summarily through the evolution of the Latin verb *meditari*. In classical Latin *meditari* means to think about something constantly, ponder, or reflect (as later in Descartes); it also has the sense of contemplating a course of action, devising, planning, rehearsing, or exercising. A *meditatio* (a meditation) is consequently a type of thinking, a mental exercise or practice. Ancient and Hellenistic spiritual exercises occasionally included reading, as in the case of Epicurus's letter to Menoeceus and the *Therapeutae* described by Philo of Alexandria, but it was in late and medieval Latin that *meditari* was most frequently associated with the verb *legere*, to read. The writers who made this connection, such as Augustine, Gregory the Great, Isidore, and Bede, were heirs to a system of meditation through reading whose roots were not only in Greco-Roman spiritual exercises but also, and perhaps principally, in the asceticism associated with Judeo-Christian biblical studies. As Jean Leclercq remarked, "In Christian as in rabbinic tradition, one cannot meditate on anything else but a text, and since the text in question is the word of God, meditation is the necessary complement, almost the equivalent, of *lectio divina*."[4] In late antiquity and the early Middle Ages, the term *meditatio* retained its links with the sense of the Hebrew root *haga*, which means to murmur in a low voice or to recite at a barely audible level. In time, the meaning was expanded to include writings that were recited or repeated from memory, passages of texts that appeared in visions, dreams, and prophecies, and, most originally, moral lessons whose significance was transmitted by images. Well before Gregory the Great summed up patristic views in 599 and 600, stating that images in churches could serve as texts for those who could not read, it was customary for Christian thinkers in both Greek and Latin to associate present or remembered images with the biblical passages whose meaning they illustrated.

An important feature of Christian meditative reading concerned the use of silence. When medieval authors spoke of *lectio et meditatio*, they referred to oral reading that was followed by silent meditation.

In chapter 48 of the Rule, St. Benedict warned monks that reading might interfere with the silence necessary for meditation because it created unnecessary noise. Silence was considered to be an integral part of sacred reading, just as oral reading was the entry point to meditative silence. This type of silence should not be confused with silent reading, which became widespread only in the century or so before the age of print;[5] in classical and late Latin such practices are usually indicated by a qualifier, as in the expression *legere tacite*, used by Augustine when he observed Ambrose reading without moving his lips.[6] By contrast, meditative silence did not consist in the absence of sound (along the lines in which contemporary society considers leisure to be the absence of work). In Augustine, and especially in Gregory the Great, meditative silence implied a nonperceptible presence: the absence of sound, which is perceived by the senses, was a confirmation of this presence, since the text of the Bible, in which divine being was thought to reside, was silent until it was read, and silent again after the oral reading was finished and the meditation had begun. To proceed from *lectio* to *meditatio* was thus to ascend from the senses to the mind.

In addition to providing the material for reflection, reading admirably concentrated the senses of sight and hearing on an inner object. This concentration was the psychological precondition for meditative experience. In the prayer that begins book 10 of the *Confessions*, Augustine says: "Confessio . . . mea, deus meus, in conspectu tuo tibi tacite fit et non tacite. Tacet enim strepitu, clamat affectu" (My confession, my God, in your presence, is made before you both in silence and not in silence: it makes no noise that can be heard, but it cries out loudly with affection).

In monastic authors after the eleventh century, who largely continued to work within the traditions of prayer of the patristic age, the combination of reading and meditation created inward reflections out of which eventually arose the self-awareness associated with a reading culture. André Wilmart, who first studied this corpus of writings, saw a specific role for written meditations, remarking that, in contrast with oral prayers composed after 1100, they contain more "personal reflections and expressions."[7] In developing meditation as a literary genre for personal devotions, medieval authors doubtless anticipated the age of the Western reader and prepared the way for its arrival. But the different objectives of the two periods should not be confused. Medieval devotional reading

was not envisaged as an autonomous activity. As oral discourse reading was related to speech, and, as silent discourse, it was an aspect
of thought. The notion that reading constitutes a subject in itself
only made its appearance with modern instruction in literate disciplines in the postmedieval period. Since the eighteenth century,
the autonomy of reading has been strengthened by the connection
between the concepts of reading and literary criticism. For medieval thinkers reading was rarely an end in itself; most often it was
conceived as a means to an end, which was the creation of a contemplative state of mind. This dimension of medieval reading practices
is well explained in the first treatise devoted specifically to reading
in the Latin West, the *Didascalicon* or *De Studio Legendi* of Hugh of
St. Victor, written in the 1120s.

One of the privileged partners of silence and contemplation in
religious reading was allegory. It is not a coincidence that the dates
of the popularity of medieval allegory correspond more or less to
the most important period of contemplative reading in the West.
The modern reader tends to understand the allegories written between Prudentius and Dante as a literary genre, but during the
Middle Ages allegory was also considered to be the literary representation of a contemplative practice, as one sees clearly in Augustine's dialogue with Reason in the *Soliloquies* or Boethius's with Philosophy in the *Consolation of Philosophy*. Allegory was one way among
others of filling the mental space created by contemplative silence.
Moreover, it was a technique that could be employed with both
secular and religious texts, since in both cases there was an alterna-
tion of sound and silence. During these brief interludes, mentally
recreated personifications clarified the role of moral, emotional,
and psychological forces in the individual's ethical orientation. Allegory thereby took part in the late ancient and medieval discussion
of self-knowledge (even if it played a minor role in the medieval literature of the cognitive sciences, which was largely indebted to Aristotle). In the Platonic allegorical narratives written between Alan of
Lille and Dante, as in the commentary of Bernard of Clairvaux on
the Song of Songs, the interior discourse of allegory became a new
literature of mystical contemplation. In Petrarch, it evolved into the
classic manner for expressing the tensions between interior and exterior in modern lyric poetry.

If medieval allegory transported reading toward topics of contemplation little known in antiquity, saints' lives opened the field of

reading to early anthropological inquiry. Christian authors writing in both Greek and Latin envisaged a broad range of connections between the texts they read and the lives they led. The boundary between the written and lived narratives was flexible, in part because both were based on theological ideas that were originally communicated in an oral narrative. These ideas were the incarnation and the eucharist, in which the principles on which an ideal life was based were learned gradually through a series of events. The story and its ethical teachings were inseparable from the life of a person who had demonstrated his physical existence in time. It was possible to interpret the central events of Christ's life in different ways, as patristic authors undeniably did, but not to detach them fully from the historicity of that life, as a pagan author like Porphyry would have preferred. Moreover, that life-history was experienced sensorially, both by Christ and by Christians who learned about his sufferings. A habit of thinking was established concerning the imitation of an ideal life in which sensorial or corporeal factors played an important part. Growing from such roots, medieval spirituality was concerned with the body in a more direct, practical manner than were the meditative practices of the ancient world, even though medieval thinkers were no less preoccupied than the ancients with emphasizing the superior status of the mind.

A parallel development arose from the association of the sensorial elements in the reading process with the literal or historical sense of the text that was read. A type of mimesis or *imitatio* took shape in which the Platonic notions of original and copy were supplemented, even at times supplanted, by the relationship between historical individuals in narrative time. The emphasis on the corporeal in medieval spirituality even made it possible for a form of life to be transferred from literary model to lived experience without the intervention of a written text. An ancient exemplar of this type of literary mimesis was the story of Anthony, who was reported by Augustine to have interpreted the gospels correctly "without a knowledge of letters."[8] Anthony's behavior, rather than anything that he said or wrote, became the text onto which the gospel narrative was inscribed. The point was not lost on Augustine when he reinterpreted Anthony's story in the account of his own conversion in *Confessions* 8.12. An original feature of this and other conversion scenes in the autobiography arises from Augustine's apparent refusal to differentiate, at least at the level of literary genre, between a narrative like the *Vita Antonii*, which he read in Evagrius's translation, and the narrative of his own earlier life, which he reconstructed from memory, since in his perspective both possessed a literary dimension and a potential audience. Augustine implied that a scenario or a schema, as it is known in cognitive psychology, could exist simultaneously in mental, linguistic, or behavioral forms, depending on the subject's disposition and the circumstances.

Interior narratives thereby became intentional narratives. After Augustine, there was a widespread recognition of the principle of literary intentionality in late ancient and medieval thought. It was assumed that an internally developing but unwritten narrative could be brought to bear on the venerable question of how a person should live a good life, with the result that the living of the life came to resemble the literary process by which an autobiography might be written. A celebrated illustration of this principle is found in the life of Francis, which claimed, citing the precedents of the gospel and Anthony, that the saint was "illiterate and without instruction" (*sine litteris et idiota*). Another expression is found in the *Book of Showings* of Julian of Norwich, written in 1373, in which the anchorite claimed that she was "a symple creature vnlettyrde leving in deadly flesh"[9] (a simple and uneducated creature, living in mortal flesh). This assertion concerning unletteredness was made at the beginning of a mystical treatise that has been judged by its editors as the finest prose written by an English woman before the appearance of the modern novelists. Still another example was the notion of *imitatio* in Thomas à Kempis, who was born some seven years after Julian wrote. Through the Devotio Moderna in which he was educated, ancient and medieval meditative practices were subsequently transmitted to humanist thinkers like Erasmus and Thomas More, whose aim was to reinterpret the ancient tradition of a philosophy of life in a form in which the principles could be derived from Christian humanism. These two authors present a less cerebral approach to the question of how one should live an ideal life than Cicero, Seneca, Marcus Aurelius, or the young Augustine: they ask their readers to take up a life of philosophy without necessarily becoming philosophers themselves.

In these endeavors, an interest was shown not only in the body, in contrast to ancient philosophical traditions, but in the emotions that accompanied the body through time. Medieval thinkers knew that emotions, like images, are communicated more democratically than the ideas contained in writings. In later ancient and medieval holy lives, it is frequently changes in emotions that mark the stages of the narrative rather than historical events or intellectual concerns. The medieval audience of the gospels, regardless of its members' level of education, was unable to consider Christ's story as a way of life without taking into consideration the moral hierarchy of the emotions the story implied, in which sentiments such as humility, meekness, and charitable love predominated. The gospel stories thereby furnished a constructive representation of the emotions that prepared the way for medieval allegorical narratives involving the virtues and vices. Let us recall that for the ancients the adoption of a philosophical lifestyle usually implied the control of the emotions by reason. The Hellenistic schools differed in the manner in which control was exercised but shared the view that emotion was inferior to reason. Late ancient authors began the slow reassessment of the role of the affective life in the creation of an ethical identity that was to continue into the early modern period. During the Middle Ages and Renaissance the imitation of an ideal life was frequently reinforced by a narrative of the emotions, that is, by a story in which the events consisted in a series of consecutively arranged and subjectively maintained mental states.

In addition to emphasizing the role of the body and the emotions in spiritual growth, medieval authors differed from their ancient predecessors in making rather more modest claims about the nature of self-knowledge. It was one thing to assert the existence of the self through the *cogito*, as Augustine did: it was a different matter to state that the self was autonomous, as ancient and modern thinkers implied. In this respect the Cartesian *cogito*, which reinstates the theme of autonomy, is perhaps both richer and poorer than its Augustinian predecessor, which stresses the benefits and limitations of the acquired self-knowledge. The conditionality of Augustine's position is summed up in the prayer at the beginning of book 2 of the *Soliloquies* in the words, "Nouerim me, nouerim te" (Let me know myself, let me know you). On this view, the knowledge of the self is always contingent. Ancient meditation attempted to teach the individual self-reliance, on the assumption that a genuinely ethical lifestyle could be attained by a few people. By contrast, its purpose in Augustine and his medieval admirers was to convince the believer that this view is a dangerous misconception. As a consequence, the medieval thinkers who adopted Augustine's viewpoint may have lived in the hope of knowing themselves better, but they did not entertain illusions about truly knowing themselves adequately. If they were strict Augustinians, in anticipation of Pascal, they perhaps believed that God could know them fully without necessarily leading them to betterment through a knowledge of themselves.

For many Christians, as well as Jews and Muslims, the denial of the autonomy of the self was a matter of faith. For Augustine, it was also a consequence of a philosophy of language. He was convinced that the knowledge that we have of ourselves depends on language and memory. Knowledge is created in our minds as words. To understand what words mean, we need the aid of memory, since syllables are sounded out one after another in a sequence both in actual speech and in the mental speech by which the meaning of a word is recreated in the mind, as he illustrated in his account of time's duration in *Confessions* 11. Furthermore, words are only signs: *deus* means "God," but the word is just a sound (or a group of letters), not the reality. A spoken word, as it is experienced through the senses of hearing or sight, is thus an indication of a reality with which it has only an indirect connection. If such signs are all that we have to work with, we can work with them endlessly without discovering any sure information about the true nature of our inner lives.

Augustine thus recognized the limitations of language for describing the self, and by implication the weakness of all forms of discourse, oral or written. It appeared to him that God, in creating us in his "image and likeness," held out the possibility of self-knowledge but denied us the capability of attaining it on our own. Reading and writing are forms of temporary recall; they are not lasting records. True, written texts endure while spoken words pass away, but their permanence is nonetheless illusory, since letters are only the transcript of impermanent linguistic events. Augustine believed that the passage of a human life, which takes place in time, has that same transient quality, whereas the self or the soul, because it is the copy of an eternal original, reflects God's intentions for its permanence. Furthermore, within this theological scheme, Augustine was convinced that realizing self-knowledge was a matter of both remembering and forgetting. In the latter role, the exercise is an adaptation of Platonic reminiscence in which the migration of souls from one body to another has been replaced by a type of

critical recollection, in which a morally imperfect soul is able to re-
cover its original dignity by forgetting one life and remembering
another. In St. Paul's words, the old life was put aside and the new
life was taken on. Augustine thus stood midway between the affir-
mation of the self's existence and the denial of the certainty of personal knowledge concerning the self's nature. The source for this
ambivalence was doubtless Plotinus, whose antinarrative and anti-
representational beliefs about the self were incorporated and considerably refined in Augustine's theory of signs.

*   *   *

A major revival of contemplative reading techniques took place
toward the end of the Middle Ages. Methods for meditation were
subsequently codified and transformed in the influential spiritual
exercises of Ignatius of Loyola. However, in general, the period
after the fourteenth century moved away from medieval reading
habits in two important respects. Oral reading was supplemented,
if not entirely replaced, by silent reading, which was practiced by
greater numbers of readers than during the Middle Ages. Accompanying this development, the meditative or contemplative aspects
of reading were reduced in favor of visual, symbolic, or interpretive
procedures that placed great weight on analytical understanding.

Under the influence of humanism, the educated reader learned
to appreciate accurate editions, so that ancient texts could be read
correctly, and philological methods, so that interpretations of those
texts could be justified. The meditative aspects of reading, at least
in their medieval forms, were less emphasized, except among devotional readers like Petrarch or, later, the metaphysical poets, Donne,
Herbert, and Crashaw. Later ancient and medieval meditation de-
pended on a distinction between sound and silence, that is, between
the sound of the oral reading and the silence that followed. With the
widespread practice of silent reading, the sound of the reading was
reduced to an inward murmur or disappeared altogether from aural
perception, so that only one type of silence remained—the silence
of reading itself. The history of silence thus began a new chapter,
in which the subject had the impression that reading and thinking
were a single, continuous process. For the reflective reader, the text
and the self became interdependent, as they appear to be in Montaigne.

In recognizing this transformation, Marcel Proust spoke of the rise of modern reading as "ce miracle fécond d'une communication au sein de la solitude"—the very foundation of "la vie spirituelle" ("that fruitful miracle of communication in the midst of solitude"—the very foundation of "the spiritual life").[10] If these words have a nostalgic ring, it is not because we still look on the Middle Ages through the eyes of the Romantics, but because we are aware that the century of Proust was the period in which literary studies finalized its detachment from traditional Western methods of relating literature to the problem of self-knowledge. Contemporary criticism has considerably obscured the relationship between reading and contemplative practice that was deliberately incorporated into many late ancient and medieval writings on the self. As a result, a new generation of readers has largely been deprived of the historical disciplines that are needed to attain an understanding of this poetry of the inner life.

Chapter Two
Ethical Values and the Literary Imagination

Ethics has for some time been a topic of interest in both philosophy and literature. One of the focal points of this interest is the ethical thought of antiquity. Much of the attention has been devoted to Plato, Aristotle, and Hellenistic thinkers down to Plotinus, who died in A.D. 270. Some notice has also been taken of the bridging figures to medieval thought, Augustine and Boethius.[1]

Students in the field are agreed that something new takes place in the late ancient period, but they are not sure what it is or how they should talk about it. The difficulty arises in part from a change in the literary genre in which ethical matters appear. There is a decline in purely philosophical discussions and a rise in the number of writings that take up ethics within secular and sacred literature. The secular philosophy of ethics virtually disappears until it is revived by Peter Abelard in the twelfth century. Yet there is a considerable deepening of relations between ethics and literary experience. This manner of presenting ethical issues breaks new ground in thinkers like Philo, Seneca, and Marcus Aurelius.

There was nothing unusual about situating ethical problems in a literary landscape. The idea was as old as Greek tragedy, the book of Job, or the Christian parables. The connection was a normal feature of Hellenistic education in grammar and rhetoric. For Cicero, who summed up ancient thinking near the end of the Roman republic, the best sort of person was considered to be an ethically informed orator, that is, someone who applied the lessons of rhetoric through participation in political life. Quintilian, writing under a different type of government, nonetheless devoted a chapter of his

influential *Institutio Oratoria* to *lectio* (1.8), where he spoke in traditional terms of literary and moral education through the study of
poetry.

Ernst Robert Curtius drew attention to the continuity in the
teaching of literature from an ethical standpoint between antiquity
and the Middle Ages, when the curriculum authors were known
simply as *ethici*.[2] However, there were no ancient prototypes for
many of the literary types of ethical discussion that appeared in late
antiquity in the form of allegory, hagiography, or confession. One
reason for the discontinuity was a greater emphasis on a reading culture, which modified, transformed, or brought about the abandonment of the major literary genre associated with ethical discussion,
the Socratic dialogue. Another arose from the ethical teachings of
Christians and Jews that were based on lessons derived from religious texts rather than from philosophical reasoning. Still another
force was the appearance of a thinker who brought together ethics
and literature in a genuinely new way. This was Augustine.

This chapter explores Augustine's contribution to literary ethics.
I should make clear at the outset that I do not consider "Augustine" and "later ancient thought" to be interchangeable categories.
Nor do I suggest that Augustine offered the only possible solution
to ethical problems in the late ancient period. My aim is to draw attention to the features of his thinking that make him a noteworthy
figure in the tradition that links ethics and literature between antiquity and the modern world. Needless to say, there are good reasons for singling out his contribution, some of which were noted in
the previous chapter. His synthesis of ancient and Christian ethics
had a long life in European letters, reappearing in a modified form
in thinkers like Petrarch and Pascal. The linguistic turn he gave to
ethics anticipated by many centuries the orientation of ethical discussion in contemporary analytic philosophy. And in the *Confessions*
he created a dramatic setting for the discussion of ethical issues that
was unequaled in Western literature before Dante.

One of the ways Augustine situated ethics within the study of
literature was through narrative. In this respect he differed little
from other Christian and Jewish authors in late antiquity. The ethical thinking that arose from these religions during the ancient and
medieval periods normally had a narrative background. In the Middle Ages there are exceptions to this way of looking at ethics, for
example, Peter Abelard, whose *Ethics* is concerned with linguistic

intentionality, or Peter Lombard, whose Sentences tackle ethical problems one by one. However, in general, the contributions to ethics during these centuries have to be viewed in the context of the pervasive medieval belief that human moral behavior was permanently altered by a set of historical events recounted in the Bible that describe the fall of mankind and its eventual redemption. To find discussions of ethics that are free of narrative considerations, it is necessary to move forward in time to Descartes's *Traité des passions de l'âme* in 1650 or John Locke's *Essay Concerning Human Understanding* in 1690.

In view of the extensive use of narrative, it is not surprising that many of the authors who talked about ethical matters in the medieval period were figures like Dante, Chaucer, and Christine de Pizan. These writers are so literary in their approach that it seems inappropriate to describe what they are doing in purely philosophical terms. Yet an assessment of their contribution to ethics as a branch of thought can be made if some generic features of their writings are kept in mind. First of all, they are more concerned with practices than with theories. Second, they take a serious interest in the patterns of the emotions insofar as these impinge on ethical issues. Finally, in their consideration of their emotional and ethical lives, they make a place for the models of correct behavior that arise in their reading of secular and sacred literature.

As a consequence, in their writings an ethical philosophy is not only a body of knowledge; it is also a set of principles that can be derived from the manner in which an ethical life has been lived.[3] In this sense ethics is a living narrative, and as a narrative it is a type of literature. It is possible to analyze one's life like a story with moral implications, and to analyze stories with moral implications as if they might have been lived.

In late ancient and medieval authors, this was typically a story that emphasized religious themes such as asceticism, the spiritual life, and the examination of conscience. The philosophical advice given in such narratives differed little from earlier, non-Christian treatises on the care or cure of the soul.[4] But there was a greater emphasis on history. The story was concerned with events, their context, and their meaning. The reliving of such a life through narrative was an exercise in interpretation. And one interpretation was connected to others. Authors who dealt with ethics in this literary manner did not think that the soul or self could exist in a vacuum, uninfluenced in any way by its surroundings. In Augustine's view, one of the sources of moral freedom is the individual's realization that people are suspended in a variety of literary webs they have willfully spun for themselves.

If such stories were told, they were presumably told for an audience that could be configured in different ways. The first audience was the author, since the story in question normally concerned the moral progress of his or her soul. The audience could likewise be understood as existing within the text, outside it, or, in Augustine's case, in a fictional space that lay between the two. The several configurations of the audience in the *Confessions* introduced a new element into the mental or spiritual exercises of later ancient ethical thinking. By engaging in a conversation that took place both with himself and with God, Augustine drew attention to the interdependence of potential audiences on matters relating to the individual moral conscience. In contrast to numerous ancient techniques for achieving the ascetic life that worked from the outside,[5] this inner dialogue questioned, among other things, the validity of its own inwardness, and thereby made it difficult for the narrator to separate the self and the configuration of the self, the self and its image, the self and its literary description.

It was not only through texts that this inner dialogue took place. Images were also involved. This aspect of the problem can be illustrated through an anecdote in Jerome Bruner's delightful book, *Acts of Meaning*. Bruner asks us whether we judge one portrait to be better than another if it more closely resembles its subject. In answering this question, he invites us to recall "Picasso's reply to Gertrude Stein's friends when they told him that she thought his portrait of her was not a good resemblance. 'Tell her to wait,' [he] said. 'It will be.' "[6] In this story Picasso acts as a witness to what has become a commonplace: the view that the relationship between the inner self and its outward representation is not something stable, objective, and enduring but is involved with changing perceptions of subject and object. Our image of ourselves consists in part of our prior mental configuration of what such an image should look like. If Gertrude Stein does what Picasso recommends—if she literally "waits" for her portrait to look more like her personal picture of herself—she will be engaging in a type of intentional thinking.[7]

The idea goes back to Edmund Husserl, to his teacher, Franz Brentano, and to earlier thinkers, among them Aquinas, Anselm, and Augustine. But Augustine expresses his concern with intentions in a rather different if complementary manner that recalls the anecdote recorded by Porphyry when his mentor, Plotinus, refused to sit for a portrait by one of his students, arguing that this would just be the image of the image of himself he had been obliged to carry around throughout his life (see chapter 3).[8] Augustine may not have known this story but he was aware of the negative attitude in Platonist thinking toward replicated images. In books 8 and 9 of *De Trinitate*, a lengthy treatise composed in the 420s in which Plotinus is quoted extensively, he approaches the issue from another angle by asking whether it would be possible to have an accurate portrait, not of a living philosopher but of a distinguished theologian who had lived in the past. The basic question concerns what can be taken to be the reality of the person in question. Augustine recognizes the importance of intentions. However, instead of speculating about the motives of someone deceased, he speaks of the purpose that arises in the mind of the portrait's creator and in the minds of the potential observers of the completed picture.

The person in question was Paul. Augustine knew that there were no accurate likenesses of the apostle. A portrait could only be created from the bits and pieces of literary description that had survived. He also knew that these did not present a consistent picture, and he agreed with the ancient view that such representations in art and literature are creative, interpretive, and usually deformative. However, he did not wish to avoid likenesses. He concluded that the identity of a person could be sought not in externals but through a consideration of his or her inner qualities, chiefly through virtues or vices. He also observed that it is we, as viewers of such a portrait, who are the final judges of its accuracy. Our judgment is based on what we know inwardly to be the qualities we are seeking, such as justice, which Augustine argued cannot be taught through external means like words or images.[9] If we do not recognize the moral qualities we associate with Paul as having an actual or potential existence in ourselves, we will not be able to understand what they may have represented in his life, or, for that matter, in anyone else's. When we reflect on Paul's character, therefore, we create an internal portrait of the apostle, and such a portrait is created first and foremost for a single audience, which is ourselves.

The canonical statement of Augustine's views on ethics and self-representation has always been assumed to be the *Confessions*. But an earlier account is found in a series of dialogues he wrote between 386 and 391.

It is here that he concludes that it is impossible to separate ethics and the language of ethical discussion. He thereby becomes a pioneer in linguistic philosophy. Two dialogues written respectively in 387 and 389 are important in the development of his position. In the earlier work, *De Musica*, book 6 contains a lengthy discussion of the reasons why judgments are never free from sense impressions. In the later work, *De Magistro*, Augustine proposes that language is a limited instrument for understanding reality. His argument is equally valid for the words we use to understand things for ourselves and the words we use to communicate our thoughts about things to others. Taken together, this pair of writings questions the ability of humans to achieve objectivity on any ethical issue that is conveyed by words (in contrast to revealed ethical truths, which are only put into words by God so that they can be understood by users of human language). Augustine takes the skeptical view that all types of ethical discourse, philosophical, narrative, or whatever, are nothing more or less than words. No literary genre, as a genre, has a special claim to truth. The use of language in ethical discussion is essentially pragmatic.

Second, within his literary and linguistic reconfiguration of ethical debate, Augustine introduces some new uses for rhetoric, the subject of his professorship in Milan until his resignation in the summer of 386. One of the traditional features of rhetorical instruction consisted in training law students to envisage themselves speaking before their intended audiences, even though those audiences would often have to be imagined. Augustine believed that all ethical statements contain an element of this type of rhetoric. As a consequence, if we want to improve our ethical thinking, we should not look to the rhetoric of performance, since we all try to use language persuasively, whether consciously or not. Instead, we should reconceive the audience of our ethical statements. It is possible for us to address our remarks to an interlocutor whose ethical understanding is presumably at a higher level than ours. We can do this because the remarks we direct outward are in response to our understanding of a position that differs from our own, even if both the statement and the response take place within the mind. If we assume that the other party is our ethical superior, then our thinking will be raised toward that level. Augustine experimented with this type of discourse in the neoplatonic prayer that opens the *Soliloquies* and brought it to maturity in the magnificent prayer that begins book 10 of the *Confessions*. In these devotional statements, his religious thoughts are elevated by the implied presence of God, just as his early rhetorical exercises achieve their success through the imagined presence of wealthy patrons like Romanianus.

The third topic on which the dialogues shed some light is the potential connection between ethics, emotions, and personal narratives. Augustine believed that all stories work in much the same way, whether they are tales we think, tell, or live. Stories achieve their ends because they work on our emotions, whose influence on behavior depends on our interpretation of the narratives to which we are exposed. Augustine did not accept the ancient view of emotion and reason as opposed forces within the soul. He was not convinced that emotions are always irrational; in his view they could contribute to ethically informed, rational action, even if human reason is never entirely free from the sensory influences that impinge on our feelings. The way we respond to emotions depends on whether memory, which records emotional experience, is the slave of habit, as he puts it in *De Musica* 6, or whether our recollections promote self-mastery through the redirection of their raw material, as he argues in *Confessions* 10. Augustine's approach may have been anticipated by the Stoic view that images of the past and the future should be avoided because of their impact on our emotions.[10] However, it was in the neoplatonic form in which he framed the issues that the connection between memory and emotion was passed on to the Middle Ages and the early modern period.

Around 401, toward the end of the period in which he was working on such matters in the *Confessions*, Augustine was involved with another problem that was central to his personal search for ethical redefinition: how to combine what he had learned from ancient philosophy with his interest in scripture as a vehicle for conveying divinely inspired truths. As a result of this inquiry, he developed not only formal links between ethics and literature but a personal attitude toward himself as a reader of religious texts. This aspect of Augustine's intellectual evolution, I believe, is unique in the later ancient world. Had he been a philosopher or a religious thinker alone, he would have occupied a minor if respectable position in the history of late ancient thought. It was his combining of philosophical interests, derived from his reading of ancient texts, with the reconfiguring of himself through his experience of biblical literature that made him truly unusual. He achieved this remarkable synthesis in part by introducing a concern with subjectivity into his deliberations. He expressed this subjectivity by creating a literary portrait of himself as a reader and a writer. As time passed, and the world of the dialogues ceded to that of the priesthood and the active bishopric, it was the literary configuration of the reader, commentator, and preacher that became his preferred model for the reflective self.

The type of withdrawal about which he had learned through his study of Plotinus could thereby be transformed into a mental instrument for distancing himself from the intellectual engagements he inevitably had to deal with in his reading and conversation. An early illustration of the technique is found in *Epistle 3*, which was a reply to his friend, Nebridius, who had come to the distressing conclusion that true happiness is unattainable, since timebound mortals are incapable of immortal wisdom. As Augustine reread Nebridius's letter before going to bed one evening, he entered into a mental dialogue on the topic. This was a method of thinking and a literary genre that he brought to maturity in the *Soliloquies*, in which the allegorical personification of Reason takes part in a dialogue within his mind on the uses and limits of reason. As *Epistle 3* suggests, it was his activity as a reader rather than other types of mental exercise that directed his thinking toward inner conversations. He later concluded that while he was engaged in reflection his thoughts on any given subject existed as mental words whose meaning could not be separated from their flow through his mind in a sequence of imaginary sounds. This sequence presented what seemed to him to be an appropriate explanation of his subjective awareness of the passage of time. He reasoned that something similar must take place when he read a passage of the Bible, and that God himself was responsible for his insight into the nature of time by imparting his eternal word to humans in the form of a linguistic and literary narrative. His consciousness of himself as a reader likewise contributed to a novel solution of one of ancient philosophy's intractable problems, namely, how a mental representation of any kind could inform the lived experience of a philosopher's life. For Augustine, this too was a question of time and narrative.

Augustine's experience differed in this respect from that of other reflective thinkers in antiquity, for example, Epictetus, Seneca, or

Marcus Aurelius. There is little about reading and writing in these figures, and what there is consists of casual statements, after-thoughts, or isolated expressions, whereas Augustine deliberately talks at length about literary activities. He included autobiographical statements among the records taken down by secretaries for study by the group of friends and relatives assembled at Cassicia-cum. It is clear from these personal insertions, as well as from his attitude toward self-reporting in the *Confessions*, that the classical problem of the progress or education of the soul had become inseparable in his mind from the education of the Christian reader. It is possible to see anticipations of this sort of thinking in Plato's *Republic* or *Laws*, which are presumed to have been read because they are too long to have been performed,[11] or in the alleged use of precomposed "confessions" in Epicureanism,[12] but the late ancient examples of implicit readership in works like Seneca's *Moral Epistles* and Augustine's *Confessions* are more self-consciously literary than anything previously written in philosophy. As soon as Augustine's personal, phenomenological style appears, the place of reading and writing in confessional autobiography is changed for good. So is the landscape of ethical discussion through literature.

Augustine believed that in order to narrate a convincing story about oneself, the narrator had to convey some idea of the type of "reality" that storytelling implies. Accordingly, as noted, in the first nine books of the *Confessions* he looked back some thirty years and told the story of how he wandered from one philosophical or religious school to another without finding the answer to the moral problems with which he was preoccupied. In books 10 to 13, he offered his readers a critique of what story and memory can teach us about ourselves. Profiting from his experience, he drew attention to what remains undiscovered and perhaps undiscoverable about the self, and he contrasted our search for this type of knowledge with what is presumably known to a higher intelligence. (It was through this negative reasoning that he arrived at the conclusion, later re-used by Anselm of Canterbury, that a supreme being is both necessary and incommensurable.) His convictions on this matter led him to a rather austere doctrine of grace, in which men and women can do little to further their own salvation on their own, least of all by telling stories to themselves. However, the same pessimism helped him to avoid a literary version of Pelagianism, by which he might have been led to believe that an author can contribute to his eternal life through the perpetual memory established by his writings.

Augustine did concede one point. He believed that storytelling, while limited in what it can tell us about ourselves, is one of the features that defines us as humans. We are "narratizing" beings because we think through words. To appreciate the subtlety of his reflections on this subject, we must not only think of a story in contemporary terms as a connected narrative, although that is one of the ways in which it appears in his life history. What he had in mind is something more basic about narrative in a linguistic sense: this is the manner in which thoughts, transformed into sequences of words, form meaningful sentences that allow narratives to be communicated from one person to another in speech or writing. It is from those strings of sounds, as little narratives, that bigger narratives are produced. In advancing this view, Augustine asked us to think of the self as inconceivable without narrative, while he denied that this narrative can convey anything essential about the self. The self that we know, therefore, as contrasted with the self as it exists, is a fictive, imaginary, or fabricated self. It is a temporary affair, like speech itself.

In view of Augustine's doubts concerning the ability of language to convey truths directly, we are entitled to ask whether the individual is meant to place confidence in stories about the self that are invented or told. In answering this question, Augustine diverged from earlier thinkers, as he did in his approach to emotions and memory. Plato believed that stories are only likely accounts of reality. Aristotle did not put much trust in stories either, unless his notion of process can be considered a kind of naturalistic narrative. Their views were echoed by many later thinkers, including Plotinus. By contrast, Augustine believed that narrative has some value because he was convinced that humans have nothing but verbal or imagistic narratives to work with when they want to talk about themselves. He blamed historical circumstances for this situation (much as we would nowadays blame genetic inheritance). In his view, narrative is a way of talking about the transformation of thought into discourse, but, as noted, it is also a way of indicating the limitations of language and human understanding for talking about the self, whose ethical reality lies beyond words in silence, as Wittgenstein observed in an Augustinian moment at the end of the *Tractatus*.

Augustine saw proof of this second point in the fact that narratives are indeterminate. As Graham Greene observed (possibly echoing a chapter of *Confessions* 11): "A story has no beginning or end: arbitrarily one chooses that moment of experience from which to look back or from which to look ahead." As we look back or ahead, is the choice our own? The novel from which I am quoting, *The End of the Affair*,[13] suggests not, and this is an accurate reflection of Augustine's view on one issue, the literary consequences of free will. In telling his story in the *Confessions* but doubting that it is the whole story, Augustine implied that freedom of the will is a question of the observer's perspective on events. The knowledge on which the viewer's decisions are based is not fully accessible: the choices are made by a being that differs from him in the way in which the time that flows by as he hears a sentence differs from the timelessness in which the meaning of that sentence seems to arise. As a result, the individual may tell a plausible story, as Augustine does in *Confessions* 1 to 9, but through the process of telling he never gets to the bottom of anything that is essential to selfhood.

Augustine was nonetheless convinced that our periodic self-reports are small steps upward in a better understanding of ourselves. He clarified his position in the introduction to his literal Genesis commentary, where he wrote a few paragraphs on the hermeneutics of biblical narrative. He suggests by implication that we should think of our personal narratives not as finished stories but as instructive episodes in which what we say about our past, if incomplete, serves as a basis for what we want to become in the future, provided that we are willing to leave that past behind, as Paul suggested, and live in an ethical and existential present. Augustine's view of the way we should live our lives and the way we should conceive the nature of time were therefore in harmony. In *Confessions* 11 he proposed that the present has no existence, since it is all past or future; yet, if the intentional role of narrative is to be realized, the present is everything, since the anxiety about the possible unreality of the self is felt and relieved in the present. For Augustine, this is a meditative present, that is, a *presence* that absorbs and dissolves all fragmenting time zones. Whether or not we follow the bishop of Hippo on this mystical step into self-awareness, we can appreciate the manner in which he connects intentions and ethics through narrative. In his view, the individual's improvement is brought about by an internal comparison of two stories, one directed toward the future, the other toward the past. An intentional story describes the self as it should be, while an already related story describes the self as it was. It is during the period of reflection on these stories that the subject addresses the critical problem of how to transform thought into action.

This is a rhetorical exercise in the positive sense in which that phrase can be understood in antiquity, as ethics presented in a genre of self-persuasion. As such, it is committed thinking. In Augustine's view there is no such thing as an ethically neutral story about oneself. We are always arguing in favor of one interpretation of events and against another. We are continually in dialogue with ourselves. As a consequence, theory in itself is not much help. In the situation in which we find ourselves, in which our thoughts are constantly shifting between past and future, between regret and desire, there is no use pretending that we can put abstract ideas in the place of historical events, as if we had possession of concepts that were applicable in all times and places. If the stream of time is a reflection of how narratives function, and if the flow of words in a narrative is an illustration of how time can be understood, then intellectual schemes for understanding behavior are not detachable from the lives we have lived or would like to live. Nor is it important in this scheme that the lives in question be our own. They can be narratives we have heard or read about, in which the ethical value of the story has been agreed on by communities over time. In such stories it is the collective hearers' or readers' response that shapes the individual's intended narrative, as it is in the life histories of the virtuous philosophers, the Jewish prophets, and the apostles.

Finally, for Augustine as for his ancient predecessors, it is not enough to hear, read about, or reflect on those lives. As noted, the narrative has to be a lived narrative. Within that program the text of philosophy functions as the record of a verbal interchange in which the possibilities of a renewed life can take shape, as it does for the participants in *De Ordine*, in which the discussion continually turns from principles of order in the world to methods for the moral ordering of their lives. The narrative books of the *Confessions*, in which Augustine completed his outline of this approach, may have been read before a live audience in the manner of an ancient epic poem, in which the hearers were invited to envisage the parts in relation to the whole while trying to recreate the conditions of living praxis out of which it arose. Augustine's philosophical goal, insofar as it related to the self, was not to construct a system but to give the individual some guidance in reorienting himself or herself in relation to others. Philosophy in this sense was a way of knowing and living, not an abstract body of knowledge.

A fundamental change in this approach occurred at the end of antiquity, through which the oral (or occasionally the silent) reader replaced the oral speaker, dialoguer, or lecturer as the typical figure who studied, meditated on, and rewrote ancient philosophical doctrine—for instance, the Augustine in book 7 of the *Confessions* whom we perceive sitting alone in his study as he compares texts of the Bible and Plotinus in search of philosophical and theological truth.[14] This sort of person increasingly became the norm as the ancient philosophical school gave way to the monastery, the cathedral school, and the Islamic or Jewish center of learning in the Middle Ages. As the oral representation of the text was replaced by the actual written text, linguistic intentionality began to exist side by side with literary, textual, and hermeneutic intentionality, although, as noted, it is easy to exaggerate the presence of these aspects of interpretation before the twelfth century. The oral likewise came to exist alongside the written without replacing it in an evolutionary fashion, as it did in the later Augustine, who effectively read and preached from written texts but spoke of his activity in terms that recalled rhetorical theories of spoken language.

Slowly, as well, ethical issues were reshaped. Among ancient philosophers, such questions were frequently articulated within a community of speakers whose ongoing debate was part of the solution to the problems at hand. The typical ancient conflict between individual happiness and community virtue was envisaged as being resolved in a manner in which positions were put forward by speakers who were conscious of their hearers and their potential reactions, since their philosophical views were often known in advance. In Augustine and thinkers afterwards, the reader was often alone with the text, except at times of liturgical or collective reading. The community was envisaged abstractly as other readers of the same text. The creation of this implied audience of readers meant that in some sense the intentionality that informed ethical thinking for the speaker had become the intentionality of the reader.

Inevitably, as well, there was a shift in interest from ethical problems that were concerned with personal happiness and the pursuit of virtue to those that were concerned with communities involved with charitable love. One of the solutions to ethical problems frequently proposed by ancient thinkers was simply for the individual to adopt a virtuous way of life. For the silent, monastic, ascetic reader of the following centuries, divine reading was in a sense that way of life. A goal of ancient philosophy had been achieved, not through a doctrine but through a mode of thought that saw self and text as self and other; a mode that reinterpreted philosophical estrangement as hermeneutic distance, and thereby provided a new avenue to the inner subject. The isolated reader lacked a way of achieving what the ancient dialogue achieved naturally: togetherness, a brotherhood of ideas, a community of thought. This is perhaps one of the reasons charity later emerged as a theological imperative as well as a literary objective in the Middle Ages.

Chapter Three
Later Ancient Literary Realism

The finest tribute that can be paid to a scholar by those who have the privilege of a historical perspective on his achievement is to renew and develop his thinking. One of the past century's scholars in the field of Latin and Romance philology who has continually inspired this type of reconsideration is Erich Auerbach.

This chapter is an attempt to broaden the context of scholarly reflection on some issues that arise out of *Mimesis*, chapters 2 to 4, and *Literary Language and Its Public*, chapters 1 and 2.[1] These chapters, which are devoted to late Latin antiquity, are among the least accessible of Auerbach's critical statements to contemporary readers. Yet their importance in the consolidation of his outlook is unquestionable. Taken together, they offer a foundation for his views on continuity and discontinuity in literary history, and through his study of Vico, on his broader perception of cultural change.

My remarks are limited to the period between Tacitus (A.D. 55–120) and Gregory the Great (ca. 540–604), and within that time span to a critical hundred and fifty years from around the end of the third to the beginning of the fifth century. In the background of what I have to say is Auerbach's view that during this period the Jerome translation of the Bible was looked on by many Christian authors as a Latin text in its own right as well as a translation from Greek or Hebrew. The Vulgate, as it became known, thereby played a part in shaping the stylistic conventions and literary outlook of a number of late Latin authors, including Augustine. In adopting this innovative viewpoint, Auerbach helped to set up stylistic guidelines for writing the literary history of the patristic age. Using Eduard Norden's *Antike Kunstprosa*[2] as a point of departure, he mapped a territory on the frontier between theology and style, especially in two remarkable essays, "Figura" (1939) and "Sermo humilis I–II" (1952, 1954).[3]

Given his interests, less is said about Greek texts and their transformation in the Latin West. This neglect may have been responsible for a weakness in his treatment of the Latin Middle Ages, namely, the insufficient attention paid to the role of allegory in authors like Prudentius, Johannes Scottus Eriugena, Alan of Lille, and Dante. In general, Latin authors whose style and methods are indebted to Greek exemplars are not singled out for special attention in his critical writings (e.g., Horace, Cicero, the young Augustine). It is legitimate to ask what happens to Auerbach's interpretive scheme when issues in Greek thought are introduced.

In what follows, I briefly examine some themes in a Greek work, Porphyry's *Life of Plotinus*, which deals with issues that reappear somewhat transformed in a text that has become well known through the quotations in Auerbach's *Mimesis*. Then I have a second look at the Latin text from Augustine's *Confessions* on which Auerbach's analysis is based. In conclusion, I hazard some observations concerning the role of the outsider in setting up stylistic boundaries for "representations" and "reality" in the late ancient period.

*   *   *

Specifically, my discussion concerns the relationship of Augustine to one of his acknowledged sources, Porphyry.

Auerbach recognized Augustine's central role in the creation of Western literary realism, in theory as well as in stylistic practice. However, he did not seek the sources of Augustine's outlook in the authors whom the bishop of Hippo read, studied, and used as a point of departure for his own speculations. Porphyry is one of several such figures who make no appearance in either *Mimesis* or *Literary Language and Its Public*.

Porphyry was the editor and biographer of Plotinus, the disciple of Ammonius, who lived between 205 and 270. He published his master's philosophical writings sometime between 301 and 305, rearranging the corpus into the six *Enneads*, that is, "groups of nine," as they are known today. It was a selection of these together with the now vanished writings of Porphyry himself that Augustine read in Milan in the spring of 386 in the Latin translation of the rhetorician Marius Victorinus.[4] Plotinus and Porphyry were largely responsible for turning him into a Christian Platonist under the tutelage of Ambrose, just prior to his conversion to the religious life.[5]

The contrast between the data of the senses and the mind that is common to Platonism and neoplatonism is the chief philosophical force shaping Augustine's notions about the literary perception and expression of "reality." Among the philosophical influences at work in introducing this distinction into his thought, a critical role is played by a combination of the ideas of Plotinus and Porphyry. Moreover, there is an important chronological relationship between the evolution of Augustine's philosophical outlook and the embodiment of that outlook in a hermeneutical theory. It was only after his assimilation of Platonic views in 386–387 that he first synthesized his thinking on prefigural symbolism and other methods of interpretation in the manner in which Auerbach presented them in his seminal essay on *figura*. Signs of what was to come appear in *De Magistro* in 389 and in *De Utilitate Credendi*, which was written in the year of his ordination, 391.

The notion that "reality" exists in a nonperceptible form rather than as a phenomenal presence is well illustrated by Porphyry's portrait of Plotinus in the *Vita Plotini* (which was not a direct "source" for Augustine, although he doubtless knew some details of Plotinus's life). In the absence of a letter collection, an autobiography,[6] or other material that would provide information concerning the philosopher's life, we are obliged to rely on what Porphyry tells us about his mentor in his biography. According to this account, Plotinus was renowned as "the philosopher of his time." Yet, as Porphyry notes, he did not provide his students with many details about his life. He never talked about his race, upbringing, or native land.[7]

More important, in view of his ascetic and mystical philosophy of life, he seemed to be embarrassed by the presence of his bodily form. Porphyry illustrates the point through an interesting anecdote to which reference has already been made. Amelius, one of the members of his circle,[8] suggested that Plotinus should have his portrait painted. Characteristically, he refused, giving this reason: "Is it not enough to have to carry the image in which nature has encased us, without asking me to leave behind a longer-lasting image of the image, as if it were genuinely worth looking at?"[9] Amelius was not discouraged. He invited a well-known artist, Carterius, to attend Plotinus's lectures, which were open to the public, and taught him how to produce a mental configuration of his master. Later Carterius was able to create a portrait of Plotinus from memory.

This is an unusual statement in ancient aesthetics, suggesting that an artistic representation of a person can come about indirectly, as a byproduct of a recollected physical image. I will have something to say about it later. For the moment, let us focus on Porphyry's reason for placing the anecdote at the beginning of the *Vita*, which touches more directly on the problem I am addressing. Plotinus's response to the suggestion of a portrait is typical of his position on sensory images in general. He denies that a picture, which is apprehensible to the senses, can convey the reality of the person, which is accessible only to the mind.

If we reflect on *Mimesis*, chapters 2 to 4, Plotinus's renunciation of the sensory would seem to be different from the attitude toward apprehensible reality Auerbach sees taking shape in a number of later ancient authors, for example, in the "realistic" statements of Tacitus, Apuleius, Ammianus Marcellinus, Augustine, and Gregory of Tours. These authors all affirm some version of Platonic or neo-platonic idealism as a philosophical doctrine. Yet they appear to be fascinated with the stylistic representation of the sensory, even to the point of endowing it with an autonomous if discomforting reality of its own. This view, even if it is only expressed in a literary manner, would seem to be at odds with their professed philosophical principles.

Of course, in making such a comparison based on the *Vita Plotini*, we have to make allowances for the literary character of Porphyry's story about his master's portrait. In his view, what Plotinus's students concealed from their master in arranging to have his picture painted without his knowledge was a puerile desire for an icon, that is, a symbolic reminder of a nonmaterial presence. By contrast, the philosopher is portrayed as concentrating his thoughts on the invisible—God, the soul, and principles of conduct. The tale may be Porphyry's (or Plotinus's) way of correcting a standard error of beginning students in schools of neoplatonism, namely, the inability to get beyond the sensory to deeper levels of "reality." Plotinus's approach (if Porphyry can be trusted) is to deny the value of the memory of the body, while nonetheless admitting its existence.

By contrast, for the Latin writers whose stories fill the pages of *Mimesis* 2–4, the memory of the body is essential to any reconstruction of the real, since (in Augustinian terms) our memory of the real is inseparable from our awareness of the passage of time in which sensory reality is perceived. Augustine differs from what Porphyry tells us was the position of Plotinus, inasmuch as his aim is not to transcend the body but to overcome it, using the images in his memory as an aid. He spells this theory out in detail in *De Trinitate*, book 14. Given what we are told in the *Vita*, we cannot imagine Plotinus representing reality through a story, while, if we look forward to Augustine's thinking on the subject, we cannot imagine reality being represented in any other way than in a narrative, apprehensible to the senses through verbal signs. In Porphyry and Augustine, philosophies and styles of presentation are deliberately being played with. The question is why.

Some light is shed on the issue if we note another feature of Porphyry's *Vita*. The philosopher who refused to have his portrait painted took care to designate a literary executor, whereas Augustine offered us his self-portrait and later acted as his own editor and publisher (in the *Retractions*). Plotinus thereby ensured that posterity would know him almost exclusively through his thought. This was to represent the reality of his self in terms of abstractions.

Like many ancient philosophers, Plotinus was reluctant to set down those thoughts in writing. Porphyry, our source of information on this subject, tells us that when he took up residence in Rome in 253–254 Plotinus was fifty-nine. By that time the philosopher had personally written some twenty-one treatises,[10] but these were circulated only to a small band of followers as guides to his public lectures.

According to Porphyry, there were three reasons for Plotinus's diffidence concerning the use of the written word. He had apparently made an agreement with two other followers of Ammonius (ca. 175–242), Erennius and Origen, not to disclose their master's teachings. He lectured on his master Ammonius for some ten years without writing anything,[11] and only betrayed the pact of silence when he learned that the other two had done so.

He was an exponent of the standard method of teaching philosophy in late antiquity, which was oral.[12] In this type of instruction the texts of earlier philosophers were read aloud with a commentary that was subsequently discussed by a master and his students. Plotinus's classes consisted of such "questions and answers" (in which, Porphyry notes, there was a good deal of disorder, misplaced emotion, and needless verbiage).[13] Porphyry speaks at length of his listening audience, which, despite the diverse origins of the members, appears to have formed a cohesive group.[14] In fact, within the *Vita* we learn more about the participants in his school than we do about Plotinus himself. Our attention is directed toward the audience rather than the source of his views: this is a necessary reorientation if we are fully to appreciate Porphyry's contribution to his oeuvre. And this, I would propose, is what Porphyry wanted.

Finally, it appears that Plotinus was not a successful writer for personal reasons. Porphyry records that "when [he] had written anything he could never bear to go over it twice; even to read it through once was too much for him, as his eyesight did not serve him well for reading. In writing he did not form the letters with any regard to appearance or divide his syllables correctly, and he paid no attention to spelling. He was wholly concerned with thought."[15] Furthermore, his student remarks, "in the meetings of the school he showed an adequate command of language and the greatest power of discovering and considering what was relevant to the subject in hand, but he made mistakes in certain words."[16] Although I make the suggestion with caution, this description reads like a classic case of dyslexia, possibly one of the earliest on record.[17] Even if it is not, the account of Plotinus's psychological limitations admirably serves Porphyry's literary purposes. It was Porphyry who catalogued Plotinus's writings and rearranged them in a fashion that made it difficult to separate the two thinkers' ideas. If we recall the anecdote with which the *Vita* opens, it would appear that a set of literary works is replacing a portrait based on memory as the symbolic icon of the master. This is an indirect connection with the method brought to perfection in Augustine.

*   *   *

With these thoughts in mind, I turn to a text brilliantly analyzed by Auerbach in *Mimesis*. This is an anecdote from the so-called "life of Alypius," which Augustine incorporated into book 6 of the *Confessions*.

There are in fact three anecdotes, of which Auerbach used one: the story of Alypius's inability to resist the sensory appeal of gladiatorial matches. This story provides a vivid illustration of Auerbach's thesis concerning the rise of irrationalism in everyday life in late antiquity. In his memorable account of the passage, he sums up the issues in this way:

> Here . . . the forces of the time are at work: sadism, frenetic bloodlust, and the triumph of magic and sense over reason and ethics. But there is a struggle going on. The enemy is known, and the soul's counterforces are mobilized to meet him. In this case the enemy appears in the guise of a bloodlust produced by mass suggestion and affecting all of the senses at once. . . . Against the increasing dominance of the mob, against irrational and immoderate lust, against the spell of magical powers, enlightened classical culture possessed the weapon of individualistic, aristocratic, moderate, and rational self-discipline. The various systems of ethics all agreed that a well-bred, self-aware, and self-reliant individual could through his own resources keep from intemperance. . . . So Alypius is not overly concerned when he is dragged *familiari violentia* into the amphitheater. He trusts in his closed eyes and his determined will. But his proud individualistic self-reliance is overwhelmed in no time.[18]

Before turning to the three interlocked anecdotes, a few words are necessary concerning their place in the *Confessions* and what they tell us about narrative representation at the turn of the fourth century. By the time the *Confessions* was written, between 397 and 401, Alypius had himself converted, entered the religious life, and become bishop in Thagaste, near Hippo. His reputation for asceticism had spread as far as Italy, from where Paulinus of Nola and his wife Therasia had written Augustine in 394, asking him for the story of his life. A scholarly debate has taken place on whether that uncompleted *Vita* was the starting point for the *Confessions*—this need not detain us.[19] The important issue is the role that the stories play in changing the direction of an important segment of the narrative books. They mark the beginning of a transitional phase, in which distant persons and remote models of virtue are gradually replaced by those nearer at hand, that is, by individuals whose stories are recorded within the living memory of Augustine's own time. The climax of this development is the introduction of the life of St. Anthony in book 8.

In contrast to Plotinus, who envisages the problem of realism in terms of images, Augustine speaks of interlocking narratives. Within that context, he retains the ambivalence about the sensory that characterizes neoplatonic idealism. The point of Plotinus's retort to Amelius's suggestion of a portrait is that the soul is unknowable through outer representations. This is Augustine's position too.

But his way of getting at the issues differs from Porphyry's. Alypius, whose stories are related in book 6, is the appropriate witness to Augustine's conversion in book 8. However, he is a witness on the outside. He tells the story of the internal changes in his friend as a narrative that is understood only through what he observes taking place in his body. He does not penetrate Augustine's thoughts. In the end, Augustine has to tell him that he has decided to take up the religious life. When Alypius does the same, he too has to relate what has transpired within himself by means of words. One would expect the anecdotes about Alypius in book 6 to prepare the way for this situation. This is what they do.

The problem of gladiatorial combat does not arise in anecdote 2, to which Auerbach refers; it is recalled from the first story. Anecdote 1 is an account of a different sort: it is not delusions of the senses that are in question but the problem of other minds. The tale begins with Augustine's nostalgic reflection on the conversations he had with Nebridius and Alypius in Milan prior to his conversion in August 386, when it was he rather than his friend who was tempted by money, honors, and the prospect of a good marriage. It was during this period that Augustine read Plotinus and Porphyry, whose ideas lie in the background of the stories he tells.

Anecdote 1 takes place during the period in which Alypius was Augustine's student in Thagaste. They held each other in high personal esteem; yet, looking back on events from the vantage point of his bishopric, Augustine the author does not think that either was particularly meritorious. He was then engaged in teaching rhetoric, an activity he subsequently repudiated. This was a type of instruction designed to show his students how to deal with words, whereas, in retrospect, he remarks that had he known better, he would have offered them methods of interpretation capable of revealing Christian truths in the Bible. Alypius was irresistibly attracted to the bloodshed of gladiatorial combat. He was even neglecting his studies to the point that a promising legal career was threatened. To make matters worse, Augustine had recently quarreled with Alypius's father. As a result, Alypius was forbidden to attend class and Augustine had no opportunity to offer him moral counsel. Alypius was too attached to his mentor to obey his father literally. He appeared in class from time to time, although only as an auditor. The idea of reproving him gradually slipped from Augustine's mind: this is an apparently innocent detail, but it introduces the notion of forgetfulness into the story and thereby provides a link with neoplatonic reminiscence.

The climax of the episode came about in this way. One day Alypius entered class after the lesson had begun. Augustine was lecturing, book in hand, and had come to the point in the lesson where it was necessary to provide an example of a moral principle. By sheer coincidence, he hit on the gladiatorial games. He did not have Alypius's misconduct in mind, but his student was convinced he did, and immediately afterward mended his ways. As we know from anecdote 2, he subsequently relapsed. Augustine, who reemerged as his mentor, then betrayed the traditional role of the ancient teacher as a spiritual director. Having misled his students into taking pagan rhetoric too seriously, he embarked on a career of converting them to Manichaeism, a substitute for Catholic Christianity he had encountered in Carthage. Sensory delusion was thus introduced from another direction: it would only be overcome in book 7 through a combination of Plotinian doctrines, the opening verses of the gospel of John, and the letters of Paul.

The story is constructed around a well-known ancient *exemplum*, related by Diogenes Laertius among others, concerning Polemo, the son of Philostratus, who renounced his dissolute life and turned to philosophy after hearing a lecture by Xenocrates on the virtue of temperance.[20] Augustine knew the story; his direct source may be Ambrose, who refers to it in *De Helia et Ieiunio.* However, in Augustine the ending is different. Polemo subsequently took over the Academy and taught the benefits of taking up a philosophical way of life; Alypius merely passes from one type of illusion to another. Also, while the original has two characters, Augustine's story has only one, since Alypius is a stand-in for the author himself. Augustine too disobeyed his parents and went from Thagaste to Carthage for his education, and he was mesmerized for a time by spectacles. As the anecdote unfolds, there is a change of emphasis from other persons' lives to Augustine's life. The real subject of book 6 is his attempt and failure to achieve a literary, that is, vicarious, remodeling of his self. The story ends without Alypius knowing what is in store for him. This is Augustine's way of reminding us that God's inscrutable ways determine the course of the narrative of his life throughout the *Confessions.*

Literary representation is thus caught up with problems of knowledge and ignorance; these themes in turn are loosely connected to metaphysically oriented doctrines concerning remembering and forgetting. There are two potential sources of human ignorance in these stories: the mutual inability of minds to understand each other and the inability of individuals to understand the ways of God.

In the second anecdote of book 6, which Auerbach quotes, the same forces are at work as in anecdote 1. Nothing takes place by chance; again, the action depends on Alypius's self-delusion. But another element is added: the force of memory, not in Alypius or Augustine, but in us, as readers of the *Confessions*. Our vantage point in the story is that of Alypius's friends, who drag him off to the games to tempt him and wait to see whether he is able to resist. Auerbach overlooked the factor of memory, which is critical, I believe, for understanding the manner in which the three narratives are intertwined. They reinforce each other in Alypius's life just as the successive conversion stories of book 8 have a cumulative effect on the life of Augustine. It is in our reconstruction of the narrative in our memories, moreover, that the moral force of the stories is realized. The audience, as a group of later readers and rememberers, thereby take on some of the omniscience of the deity.

For this reason, the time frame of anecdote 2 is different, while the situation reiterates what has come before. Alypius is now in Rome, several years later, although still pursuing a worldly career and addicted to the sight of blood. The moral of the story is that Alypius should have relied on God, when he put all his trust in himself. Augustine believed that self-confident rationalism was the weak link in pagan philosophies as well as in Manichaeism. He disagreed with those who trusted in human reason to resolve the difficulties facing the individual in the moral and religious sphere. Alypius does not fail because he lacks self-discipline, as Auerbach proposed, but because he places too much faith in it. He is weak not because he is unaware of his inner life but because he refuses to seek support for it outside himself.[21] Like Augustine, he lives in what Plato and Plotinus called "a region of dissemblance."

*   *   *

This phrase, *regio dissimilitudinis*, which echoes down through the centuries after it is latinized by Augustine,[22] brings me to the final theme of this chapter. This is the status of the outsider in these accounts. If we compare the views of Plotinus and Augustine on this subject, we see a subtle transition. Understanding this change will help us to put Auerbach's contribution to the subject in perspective.

Let us begin with Plotinus. What sort of an outsider was he? Essentially, one might suggest, a person seeking an alternative lifestyle. After his training in Western philosophy under Ammonius, he appears to have embraced the religious philosophies of Persia and India—although we are not told which ones. He even tried to get to the East as a soldier. When the young emperor Gordian III was murdered at Zaitha in Mesopotamia in 244, he narrowly escaped to Antioch, returning to Rome at age forty during the reign of Philippus I (A.D. 244–249).[23] Despite his foreign origins, he proceeded to acquire a considerable following. Porphyry tells us that three senators were regular members of his entourage. One of them, Rogatianus, underwent a change of lifestyle that is typical of late ancient conversions and is echoed at a different social level by Augustine's imperial converts in *Confessions* 8.6. He renounced his property, dismissed his servants, and resigned from public office. He gave away the spacious house in which he had long dwelt and began to stay as a guest with his friends, eating a meal only once every two days (incidentally, curing himself of gout).[24] He was typical of men and women of high rank in Rome who entrusted their property to the disinterested Plotinus;[25] he kept their accounts in order, thereby freeing them from worldly matters and enabling them to devote their attention to living a philosophical life. Plotinus frequently judged disputes on their behalf, and he was said never to have made an official enemy[26]—no mean feat for an academic. He was "honored and venerated" by the emperor Gallienus and his wife,[27] who apparently supported the impractical scheme of founding a city of philosophers in the Campania to be called Platonopolis.[28]

Augustine was also something of an outsider in Rome, but his situation as a teacher was different. When he came from Carthage in the hope of better minds and higher pay, his accent gave him away as a provincial and he was frequently cheated out of his fees.[29] Later, in Milan, when he had the equivalent of a "regius chair" in rhetoric, he nonetheless remained sensitive to the social and intellectual distance that separated him from his chosen mentor, Ambrose. The well-known silent reading episode at *Confessions* 6.3 is a study in willful meditative isolation on Ambrose's part and of unwanted intellectual alienation on his. When he found himself at length in the bishop's presence, he appears to have behaved like an undergraduate who is brought before a teacher whom he longs to meet, only to find that he is too shy to articulate his deepest concerns. He had achieved the visible status of a professorship, yet he envied a beggar whom he observed in a drunken state, who had a better understanding than he concerning the simple pleasures he wanted out of life (6.6). Even in his maturity, when he wrote *The City of God*, Augustine was more at ease on the periphery than at the center of the empire. It is his conception of himself as an outsider that gives the polemical rhetoric of this great work much of its ironic force.

Porphyry takes pains to contrast the description of Plotinus's physical disabilities in old age with his otherworldly position on philosophical matters. Indirectly, the *Vita* also stresses the difference between his personal habits and his political influence. In chapter 2 we hear of a variety of ailments the philosopher endured: bowel disease, ulceration of the hands and feet, and, as death neared, the inability to lecture.[30] Yet, through his ascetic withdrawal from society, he continued to wield considerable spiritual influence to the end. He was a model to be imitated, even by persons who had only a slight grasp of the subtleties of his ideas. His alienation, in short, was not one of nationality (although he spoke Greek in a Latin world), but of beliefs. It was not imposed on him; he imposed it on himself.

The perspectives of Plotinus/Porphyry and Augustine each have their implications in the domain of representation. In Plotinus, the reality that hovers between self and otherness remains a philosophical and psychological problem for the individual. If we look forward to Augustine and beyond, the imitation of holy persons is supplemented, even at times replaced, by a certain style of model narrative. Living, reading, and writing lives have become aspects of a single process: we are halfway to Freud. The philosophical ideals Augustine implants into Alypius's stories are not so different from those Plotinus provides for the senator Rogatianus. Yet in Augustine's scheme it is these interlocking narratives that instruct Alypius and ultimately us as well. While Plotinus begins within the concept of the soul, Augustine's point of departure is the senses, above all, the senses of sight and hearing, through which narratives, as sequences of meaningful words, are understood. This is to say that, in Augustine, as in poets and prose writers who follow him down to Dante, it is aspects of the perception of the earthly world, as Auerbach elsewhere argued,[31] that are the starting point for understanding reality. As a former professor of rhetoric, Augustine refused to separate the question of narrative from that of inherited teachings on the style of oratorical expression. By this route, the problem of self and otherness, as it arose in his Platonist teachers, rejoined the issue of representation.

Augustine is not the first writer to hold such views, although he may be the first to offer a synthesis. Even here, however, other forces are at work in concert with his interpretation of the three levels of oratorical style. The chief of these is his rethinking of notions of memory, time, and the powers of the soul, which take us back by a different route to Plotinus.

In my summary of the anecdote that begins Porphyry's life of the philosopher, I postponed a discussion of the important statement about memory. Now is the time to return to it, but not precisely in the context he envisaged. To reiterate, Amelius, who taught Carterius how to paint from memory, instructed him through a type of visual mnemotechnics. This was an application of standard teaching on the art of memory.[32] Plotinus would have opposed imagism, as Porphyry says, but not the theory of memory on which it is based. In fact, what Porphyry says about recording details in the memory sounds rather like what Plotinus says about the same topic at *Ennead* 4.6.3, where he notes that "exercises to improve our mental grasp show that what is going on [in memory] is an empowering of the soul, just like the physical training of our arms and legs . . . by continuous exercise. For why, when one has heard something once or twice, does one not remember it, but [only] when one has heard it many times . . . ?" Augustine shared Plotinus's view that memory operates through an active element in the soul, not just recording sense impressions but permitting mental images to pass from potentiality to actuality. He also saw memory as the locus for reconstructed narratives, as an adaptation of Platonic reminiscence.

It was through his theory of memory that Augustine was able to transform a philosophical problem in neoplatonism into a literary problem for the West. The psychological awareness of alienation became the literary expression of alienation. A problem in the soul became a problem in narrative representation, and with it the inwardness of the mind became identified with the inner discourse of the text. There is no truly literary awareness of the issues in Plotinus, whereas, in Augustine, they are already so sophisticated in their presentation that the following centuries of literary criticism are merely a gloss on his ideas.

I would argue, therefore, that a turning point in this tradition occurs in late antiquity, one that is disguised by the continuity of stylistic development between Tacitus and Gregory of Tours. The relativism that Plotinus associates with sensory impressions in the soul reemerges as the relativism of the observer's point of view on a series of events. That is the rationale that lies behind Augustine's transformation of Plotinus's ideas in his well-known discussion of memory and time. Later writers in the West, while not reproducing the subtlety of his arguments, nonetheless perpetuated the literary tradition which they support. Auerbach saw in later ancient narrative a growing fascination with irrationalism and the cult of violence. Surely this was a reflection on his own age as much as on antiquity. The forces that he observed in the Roman period were there at the beginning as much as they were at the end. What the ancient narratives on this topic lack is not a description of evil in the world but an acceptable explanation of it. Augustine thought that he had an answer. Some would disagree: yet, in supplementing the action of the soul with the remembered action of narratives, he took Western literary theory in a genuinely new direction.

Chapter Four

The Problem of Self-Representation

This chapter, in keeping with the themes of the previous two, is an invitation to reflect on the functions of literary experience in later ancient and medieval authors who deal with the elusive notion of the self.

I begin with a few words about the attitude toward reading and writing in Seneca and Marcus Aurelius. I then turn to some medieval Latin texts that take up the theme of self-representation, including the works of Peter Abelard, Guibert of Nogent, Hugh of St. Victor, Guigo I, and the biographer of Christina of Markyate. I conclude with a note on Francis of Assisi and secular authors after 1300.

* * *

The issue I wish to raise can be brought into focus by comparing the uses of reading and writing in Seneca's *Moral Epistles* and Marcus Aurelius's *Meditations*.[1]

Seneca, who wrote around A.D. 63, takes the view that reading and writing can play a fundamental role in the search for self-knowledge and wisdom. Study is to provide Lucilius with food for thought as well as mental discipline (2.1–2). Daily readings are the preferred form of leisure (5.1). Seneca cautions his friend not to become a slave to his writing desk: reading is like physical exercise, which achieves its best results if spurts of activity are followed by periods of relaxation (15.2–6).

Few ancient authors are as forthright as Seneca in describing the pleasure of books. He opens a promised volume casually, "without meaning to do any more than get an idea of its contents," but he finds it so enjoyable that he cannot put it down. "It held my attention, and drew me on, so that I read it through without a break."[2] In principle he believes that lessons can be learned from either books or people (7.6–9), but in practice nearly everything he considers useful for self-improvement is acquired through his reading (e.g., 7.10–12). When Lucilius accuses him of avoiding a Stoic philosopher's responsibilities, he answers that his retirement has been misinterpreted. "I have only buried myself behind closed doors so that I can be of use to greater numbers of people. My time is not passed in relaxation (*otium*), but in useful employment (*negotium*). . . . I devote much of the night to study, keeping my eyes at work when they close involuntarily from fatigue. . . . I am acting on behalf of later generations. I am noting down a few things that may be of use: committing to writing helpful recommendations (*salutares admonitiones*) that can be compared to successful medical prescriptions." (8.1–2).

Marcus Aurelius approaches the exercises of reading and writing in a different spirit in his *Meditations*, which were set down a few years before his death in 180. His tutor had taught him that careful reading was preferable to clever speech (1.7). The pages of the *Meditations* bear witness to his lifelong study of the classics; on occasion, useful maxims are listed (e.g., the quotations from Euripides and Plato at 7.37–52 and 10.21, 23). Yet, working within the same philosophical tradition as Seneca, he does not give books a comparable role in his program for disciplining the mind and achieving self-knowledge. Forget books, he tells himself: the only thing that matters is one's capacity for reasoning (2.2; cf. 12.3). In his view, a person can be lacking books and even clothing and still be a philosopher, if he knows how to think (4.30).

Books have to be put aside if Marcus is to isolate himself and achieve a stable internal regime (*hegemonikón*, 2.2). By detaching itself from the outside world, his mind becomes aware of its internal powers (4.3). His higher self becomes invincible when it withdraws into itself and calmly refuses to act against its will (8.48). The goal of his engaging in philosophy is not to acquire facts but to find a pathway to "the little field of the self" (4.3, 12.7). To make this possible, the mind has to focus on the present, whereas reading invariably directs one's thoughts to the past or the future (2.2, 3.10; see also 7.2, 8.36, and 12.1). The uninstructed person is one who lacks not a literary education but the capacity for turning inward: it is this detachment that enables the soul to make itself an impregnable citadel (8.48).

Far from conferring immortality, as Seneca suggests, writing is a distraction, because it takes his attention away from his internal life. The study of the writings of others is not much help either. Even the greatest of comedies and tragedies in the ancient theater are merely imitations of nature. If Marcus wants to understand how the world is governed, he has to study nature itself (11.6, 11.10). The best teacher is his internal voice. Moreover, it is not books that he has to learn to read, but people, above all himself (11.15). In order to teach reading and writing, one first has to be a student: the same is true of life (11.29).

There is a good deal of rhetoric in these reflections on literary experience. Seneca talks about reading, but his chief interest is the person. Marcus Aurelius talks about the person, but he leaves posterity a written statement of his views that becomes a literary classic.

There is nonetheless an important difference in their approaches. In the *Moral Epistles*, the notion of the self derives in part from the literary configuration of Seneca and Lucilius as readers and writers of letters. By contrast, Marcus Aurelius keeps the literary description of himself at a distance. He believes that reading and writing are worldly activities that can alienate the individual from what is essential to the self.

It is possible that these attitudes have something to do with the audiences of the respective writings. Seneca was writing for at least one other person, whereas Marcus Aurelius appears to have written for himself alone. Seneca dictated what he had to say to secretaries; he adopted a well established literary genre, the letter collection; and he intended his correspondence to be published as a unit. The *Meditations* were in all probability written by Marcus Aurelius himself; they were unpublished during his lifetime, and, as far as we know, untitled;[3] and they were not written in a literary genre that was easily recognizable to outside readers, but rather as *hypomnemata*, that is, as notes for the author's private and personal consideration.[4]

The *Meditations* is the more typical of the period's attitude toward the use of texts in the search for self-knowledge. In general, Hellenistic and late ancient authors did not write treatises that were intended to be read systematically, as we would nowadays pore over a work of philosophy by Kant, Locke, or Hume. Written statements often functioned as transcripts of verbal discussions. Philosophers were reluctant to put their ideas into a permanent form: as noted, we should have practically nothing of Plotinus's *Enneads* if his student Porphyry had not insisted on editing and publishing them. Even when they appear in writing, the meandering reflections that are found in works like the *Discourses* of Epictetus are not easily detached from the oral style of presentation out of which they apparently arose. The audience that was envisaged in these performances was a group of persons who listened to a master as he was speaking. The purpose of verbal exposition was to argue in favor of the doctrines of a particular school of thought. The presence of friends, students, and associates at the gatherings was a sign of their interest in taking up the philosophical life as well as in the discourse that accompanied that life. In this context, the teacher was not only a professor but also a mentor and a spiritual guide.

Within this type of endeavor Seneca stands out as something of an exception, at least in his *Moral Epistles*, which were evidently written for both a real and an implied readership. The merits of this style of presentation were not lost on at least one later student of the collection, namely the author of the letters of Héloïse, who quoted with approval (and, if it was not Héloïse, perhaps with irony) Seneca's statement on the advantages of letters over pictures or memories in recreating the presence of an absent friend.[5] Whoever the author of Heloise's replies to Abelard was, she (or he) was right on one point: we have to have Seneca's letters before us, as a text to be read, if we are to understand them adequately, since the correspondence is too complicated in its organization for its arguments to be retained in the listener's mind after a purely oral delivery. By contrast, Marcus Aurelius deliberately isolated his philosophical statements so that in their disconnected form they could be thought about one by one, presumably by himself, when he did not have his transcript in hand. The written text appears to have been an afterthought. There is little or no consideration of a reading public.

These contrasting attitudes toward reading and writing were united in what is acknowledged to be the most profound inquiry into self-knowledge in late antiquity, the *Confessions* of Augustine. The bishop of Hippo does not appear to have been greatly influenced by either Seneca or Marcus Aurelius. However, like Seneca, he created a work of literature that was intended to be read, and, like Marcus Aurelius, he made considerable use within that work of the conventions of oral discourse.

Augustine also brought new thinking to traditional forms of self-analysis. He did this in large part through his theory of narrative and his precartesian version of the *cogito*. As I have remarked earlier, he believed that what we know ourselves is conceptualized and articulated in words. In order to make sense, these words have to follow one another in a sequence, as they do in a sentence; they thereby provide a mental link between narrative, memory, and time. The syllables that we utter when we create a series of meaningful sounds are understood as connected words with the aid of memory. The faculty of memory likewise permits us to distinguish between the flow of those sounds, as a temporal phenomenon, and their meaning, which appears to us to be independent of time's passage. In Augustine's view, self-understanding is similarly based on the temporal, insofar as it uses language, and the nontemporal, insofar as it arises from our awareness that we are thinking. Through the *cogito*, we can say that there is something that we know for sure, whereas through the knowledge that arises from language, there is very little if anything that is not subject to doubt. Augustine thus agrees with previous thinkers who maintain that the mind is incapable of knowing itself in full. Yet, viewed positively, this limitation is proof that our minds have capacities that are not bound by the rules of our own thinking.

*   *   *

Despite their different approaches to literary experience, Seneca, Marcus Aurelius, and Augustine were united in the view that the activities of reading and writing are not ends in themselves. They are means to an end, the making of a better person.

This attitude was widespread in philosophical and theological writing in the Middle Ages. However, toward the end of the eleventh century, another way of looking at the literary presentation of the self made its appearance. In this approach, reading and writing were not primarily viewed as spiritual exercises. Nor was the purpose of engaging in literary activity the moral improvement of the author or the audience. The descriptions were simply intended to convey the literary portrait of a person from one mind to another.

Medieval authors were well aware that this type of literary activity could be pursued without the consideration of higher ethical principles. Accordingly, the reappearance of such rhetorical portraits was accompanied by the awareness that, no matter how finely they were drawn, they did not represent anything very much but themselves. This tension between literary presentation and ethical considerations was an important development: it was the first phase of an internal critique that expanded along the frontiers of different literary genres and eventually reached its culmination in the universal literary skepticism of Montaigne.

Inasmuch as the tension involved the language by which the self was described, it is tempting to trace this type of thinking to Augustine, since he offered his readers an unforgettable portrait of himself in the *Confessions*. The case for Augustinian influence on the rise of literary self-representation has been strengthened by the research of Pierre Courcelle, who as previously mentioned demonstrated that the *Confessions* enjoyed a continuous readership throughout the Middle Ages and the Renaissance.[6] Augustine may have been the first person to suggest that the self can be reflected upon as if it were a literary text and that persons can "reread" themselves inwardly through the examination of the personal narratives in their memories.

Support for this approach to the problem of self-representation can be found in Augustine's theory of signs. This theory validates the use of memory, since the relationship between words and things is based on recognition.[7] It is also possible, using Augustine's theory of signs, to take a "nominalistic" rather than a "realistic" approach to representation, and as a consequence to consider the self to be a problem in language alone. Late medieval authors likewise were aware of Augustine's conviction that personal life narratives were stories whose beginnings and ends were hidden from the subject's view. If the teller of such a story wanted to analyze the events of a life beyond their literal meaning, the preferred access was the language of the moral, allegorical, or anagogical senses. The obvious model for students of Augustine was biblical narrative, whose mysteries he argued were presented in obscure language in order to test the powers of interpretation of faithful readers.

However, Augustine himself stressed the limitations of language in self-analysis. His two portraits of himself in the *Confessions*, before and after his conversion, are meant to be parts of an extended spiritual exercise rather than independent literary descriptions. If the *Confessions* is called an autobiography, as in some sense it should be, it has to be understood that the presentation of the early Augustine is largely rhetorical: its purpose is to offer a moral contrast to the Augustine who is writing the account in the first person, whose literary description we are deliberately not given. Augustine's diffidence on this matter—his refusal, in effect, to offer us a picture of what he is like as he writes, and to present us instead with sketches of himself as he evidently does not exist at the time of writing—is in keeping with the Plotinian mistrust of the capacity of words or images to convey the ideal, inner, or essential qualities of the individual. Augustine is sympathetic to this point of view; he devoted several books of *De Trinitate* to the distrust of images of the self in concert with his reading of Plotinus. In the *Confessions* he presents his position in the context of a particular life. He offers his readers images of himself that are superseded over time, one after the other. By implication, he suggests that it would be possible to have a permanent portrait of himself, but only if that image represented the person he is in the process of becoming rather than the person he is. According to his Pauline theological perspective, he will not become that transformed individual truly and permanently until the next life, when images, portraits, or likenesses will be superfluous.

This approach to words and images harmonizes with the limited role for human intentions in Augustine's metaphysics, owing to the large part played by divine providence. It was on this point that many medieval authors disagreed with their acknowledged tutor in the writing of personal narratives. They admired the way the bishop of Hippo had told his own life story, but they frequently accounted for human motivations through an extension of his ideas with which he himself would not have agreed. If narratives were constructed by the flow of words, as he had suggested, then it could be argued that personal decisions had to be understood in the first instance through an analysis of those words.

The major period of change was the late eleventh and twelfth centuries, which saw the emergence of the modern view that human thinking is chiefly characterized by intentionality.[8] This aspect of the period's interest in mental activities is widely acknowledged, but historians over the decades have not been in agreement on the context in which it should be interpreted. Medievalists in the late nineteenth and early twentieth centuries, reacting to Burckhardt, were mainly concerned with offering an alternative account of the rise of Western individualism. They saw their task as a refutation of the thesis that collectivist conceptions of the person, which had allegedly prevailed during the Middle Ages, were superseded in the Renaissance by more individualistic notions under the influence of a classical revival. A comparable stream of commentary developed out of Marx and Max Weber and dealt with the economic and social influences on the creation of a more individualistic outlook during the Reformation. The vocabulary of these early debates continues to reappear in the titles of popular studies,[9] but scholarly attention in the past generation has been redirected in large part toward the examination of the internal determinants of medieval conceptions of selfhood:[10] these include changes in religious practices, the transition from auditory to visual memory,[11] and above all the spread of a literate mentality among large numbers of clergy and laypersons.[12]

John F. Benton summed up the views of numerous commentators on the complicated question of self-representation in the twelfth century when he proposed that the period's "perceptions of individuality" were difficult to separate from the "consciousness of self."[13] I suggest qualifying these phrases with the adjective "literary," because this was the first period since antiquity when a wide range of relations between the self and literary experience were significantly rethought. Among other forces, questions of reading, writing, and intentionality were instrumental in defining the boundaries of an independent notion of the self in contrast to types of interdependency based on considerations of race, family, lineage, historical devolution, and cosmology.

What is it that characterizes what I am calling an independent self? Briefly summarized, it is a faith in the inherent separateness of persons, who are thought to be "self-contained, self-actualized, self-expressed, and self-realized."[14] More particularly, emphasis is placed on the organization of behavior in relation to the subject's thoughts, feelings, or actions, rather than to those of others. External actions are considered to be the result of internal motivations. The theme of "inner" and "outer," a development out of Paul and Augustine, attracts an increasing amount of attention; reflections on the self are largely devoted to explaining the relations between them, whether these are conceived in historical, theological, or psychological terms. As a consequence, this notion of the self is chiefly concerned with the internal attributes of the self, with its emotional and cognitive makeup, rather than with environmental forces influencing self-representation.

The independent self was not an invention of the Middle Ages but a legacy of ancient Greece and Israel that was transformed during the patristic period. While the words of Jesus on the topic of the self can be diversely interpreted, Western patristic apologists, who were indebted to pre-Christian Greek and Hebrew ideas, were united in their conception of a voluntarist faith, which implied a large degree of moral responsibility for the individual. During the Middle Ages, the notion of the self's autonomy was strengthened by the reintroduction of ancient precedents for literary individuality; the force of these notions gathered momentum between the ninth and twelfth centuries in hagiography, historical writing, and speculative theology. There was a renewal of the apostolic life, religious commitment, and the practice of confession, all of which relied on literary and theological models that stressed the individual's relationship with the divine. The negative theology that became popular through the translation of the writings of Maximus the Confessor and pseudo-Dionysius by John Scottus Eriugena reinforced notions of personal uniqueness, while agreeing with Augustine's view that the understanding of the sources of this type of individuality lay beyond humans' grasp. A typical product of this composite thinking about the self is found in Alan of Lille's lengthy twelfth-century poem, the *Anticlaudianus*, which is an attempt to write a philosophical allegory on the creation of man. Alan's perfect man, the new Adam, so to speak, is created by intellectual and cosmological forces that he does not control or even fully understand; however, through their internalization he becomes an effective ruler of nature and man. He is a new type of philosopher-king.

*   *   *

A striking illustration of the twelfth-century understanding of intentions is found in Peter Abelard. His *Historia Calamitatum* is a story of intentionally motivated decisions both by him and by others, while his *Ethics* works out a theory of the linguistic causes of intentions and their relationship to sinfulness.[15] The accounts do not fully harmonize: in the *Ethics* the value of actions is deemphasized, while, in the life history they are important witnesses to internal decisions. The autobiography is the more typical of the period's thinking on the problem of intentionality, and his reflections on this issue provide one of the ways in which the *Historia* is distinguishable from its two chief exemplars. Unlike Boethius, who sees his soul torn between fortune and free will, or Augustine, who is haunted by predestination, Abelard conceives himself as a victim of a fate that he has largely brought on himself.

The story achieves its almost contemporary atmosphere from the interweaving of several intentional narratives, in which individuals' thoughts crystallize in actions that either fulfil or deny their hopes. It is within this interpretive design that the wise Abelard, having learned the lessons of life, comments on the mistakes of his youth, and in recognition of his moral deficiencies he perceives himself worthy of the consolation of the unnamed friend to whom the *Historia* is addressed. This literary strategy is pursued in different episodes in the story, occurring, for example, in the description of his debates with William of Champeaux and Anselm of Laon. We learn little of their ideas, except through his interpretation, but we hear a good deal about their jealousy of his precocious brilliance and still more about his personal pride in his achievements in logic, which are a major source of his downfall. In a comparable fashion, Abelard presents the seduction of Héloïse as an anticipation of her emotions and as a deliberate rerouting of her laudable intellectual goals. Héloïse seems to follow the same approach in her refusal to marry, which reflects his interests rather better than hers.

The correspondence of Abelard and Héloïse is thought by some to be a forgery of the early thirteenth century,[16] but the role given to intentions is an authentic creation of the previous century and a half. An important variant in this development occurs in another autobiographical work of the period, the *Memoirs* of Guibert of Nogent, whose modernity has been the subject of considerable attention, along with his complicated admiration for his mother.[17] Guibert succeeds in extending the notion of intentionality into the fields of history, religion, and society. He has essentially one explanation for everything—the relationship, or lack of it, between the inner and outer. The historical and religious aspects of the design appear in his Genesis commentary, his treatise on relics, and his history of the first crusade. The social forces are illustrated by his *Memoirs*. The three books are linked by a social construction of events in which internal flaws in individuals and families are proposed as causes of a variety of social disasters. These include the formation of the communal movement in northwest France and the internecine murders of twelfth-century Laon. In place of the introspective self-examination of Augustine, whose *Confessions* he wistfully recalls in his first paragraph, he creates a world within his text on which he can impose an order of words rather than of things, as Augustine might maintain, in contrast to the chaos of his emotions and of political events. This emphasis on interiority is both a sign that Guibert is engaging in a spiritual exercise through a literary confession and an indication of a utopian design: it allows him to withdraw from the world, and it expresses his nostalgia for the uncluttered spirituality of the patristic age in contrast to the institutional and intellectual ferment of his own, which he clearly does not understand. Finally, let us note that his memoir, like Abelard's, is the witness to a change of another type: both personal histories are distant predecessors of *Le rouge et le noir*, inasmuch as the struggles of the mind are preferred to those of the battlefield.

Other twelfth-century autobiographical authors, such as Giraldus Cambrensis, focus on external events as influences on the internally organized representation of the self.[18] But such descriptions comprise less than half the story that this rich period tells. The majority of texts on the theme consist of spiritual or devotional works in which a subject, often speaking (or writing) in the first person, offers advice on how to attain self-understanding through the study of scripture. It is not the presence of texts that distinguishes these authors from their ancient predecessors, but the number and variety of personal expressions. They differ from early medieval contributions to the study of the self in theology and hagiography in their frequent use of writing as a complement to reading in explorations of the inner life. It is in these works rather than in the period's rare autobiographies that the connections between reading, writing, and the understanding of the self take important first steps toward the modern notion of an autonomous literary experience.

This type of spiritual exercise has one point in common with ancient techniques for understanding the self. Its vehicle is the spoken word. Silence also plays a large part, both as a sign of the absence of the speaker's or reader's voice and as an indication that a state of altered consciousness has been attained. Within this scheme, the medieval *meditatio,* which is a genre of soliloquy, gradually takes the place of the oral dialogue of antiquity, and the exercise of meditating individually on a text is eventually transformed into the early modern study of a text, which may produce a secondary text as its byproduct. Devotional reading becomes a type of reflective thinking and writing in which self and text are closely integrated.[19] The religious author who is traditionally associated with the new methodology is Anselm of Canterbury, especially in his *Orationes* and *Meditationes,* but the true originator is Jean de Fécamp, whose *Confessio Theologica* was written before 1078.

At this point it may be useful to provide some guidelines for this sort of meditation. My illustration is the brief synthetic statement in the *De Meditatione*[20] of Hugh of St. Victor. In Hugh's view, meditation has three possible objects: created things, the text of the Bible, and moral conduct (*in creaturis, in scripturis, in moribus*). The first inspires us, the second answers our questions, and the third furnishes applications in life (1, 4–7). The orientation of the self is at the center of this tripartite scheme, whose purpose is to prevent evil and encourage good (1, 2, 20–40). Meditation is "the thinking involved in our taking counsel on how to transform thought into action. For knowledge without such implementation is useless" (2, 2, 43–45). Like other types of interpretation, meditation is divisible into the historical, allegorical, and tropological (2, 3, 46–47), but its objective is a set of moral practices rather than an intellectual scheme for understanding other religious texts. Hugh is emphatic on this point, to which he devotes the largest section of the treatise, part 3, where he speaks of meditation in relation to emotions, thoughts, and works (3, 1, 64–65). He describes its effects outside the person in relation to reputation (*fama*) and within in relation to conscience (*conscientia,* 3, 2, 94–96). As a way of orienting our lives in a profitable direction (3, 5, 147–48), meditation involves the deliberate exercise of the will (3, 6, 167–68). Meditation thereby utilizes an Augustinian principle in search of the Benedictine ideal of a "form of life" (*forma vivendi,* 3, 8, 184–85).

Hugh's scheme places the self-conscious consideration of the text at the starting point of his reflections.[21] However, within the period's sacred literature, a number thinkers take a different view. A major spokesman on behalf of a less openly hermeneutic position is Guigo I the Carthusian, whose *Meditations* have the same relationship to writers like Abelard, Guibert, and Hugh as does Marcus

Aurelius to Seneca. In Guigo, as contrasted with his Stoic predecessors, the text is not really absent: it is present in its absentness. To meditate is to engage in reflection with a text in mind, one that has been read aloud and is retained in the memory while the subject's thoughts take shape. The passage read focuses the individual's attention as a precondition for meaningful contact with the inner self, but the process of thought may lead his or her thoughts in a different direction from the text's content. In Guigo, the text that is read acts as a point of departure for focusing the individual's attention on his or her subjectivity.

In addressing his thoughts to himself, then, Guigo uses a type of personal reflection that is similar to the *Meditations* of Marcus Aurelius, but he transforms it into a more self-consciously literary experience. He also modifies the Augustinian notion by which the meaning of words as they are reflected upon in the mind is conceived as mental "extension"(*distentio*). In his view, "each and every thing has its place and time in the discourse of the world (*in mundano discursu*), like a syllable in a poem" (181). The syllable, in being sounded, perishes: so does the beauty of all earthly shapes and forms; and the soul, in attempting to take hold of ephemeral things, is itself disfigured (33). Guigo likewise restates the neoplatonic preference for realities over images. If a replica of something useless is carved in gold, he argues, the material, being precious, is preferable to the image, which is taken from an object that has no intrinsic value. However, should the image of an angel be similarly engraved, the opposite would be the case: the image would be preferable to the object because an angel, being spiritual, is more valuable than even the most precious metal. By implication, if the mind is attracted by the senses, it moves away from "a rational and living substance" toward something inferior. But if it is attracted by truth, it remains "substantially" a mind, while formally it becomes divine (360).

The notion that something human can in any sense become divine moves rather far from the pessimism of the Augustinian trajectory for the narrative self. Guigo is less interested in limiting the mind through sensory confinement and God's unknowable will than he is drawn to the notion that God and man can unite in a meditative presence through the intermediary of a biblical text.[22] In this process, the image of man (or woman), if it is not actually raised to the level of God, becomes a full partner in a type of spiritual ascent. The idea is not far from Hugh of St. Victor's notion that humans can progress beyond the condition that they inherited from the garden of Eden through Christian education—another view to which Augustine had an unflinching hostility but which gained adherents during the late Middle Ages and is reflected in the Reformation by More and Erasmus. While Hugh explores the possibility through interpretation, Guigo pursues it through such vehicles as intuition, aphorism, and association.

Still another approach to the self and literary experience is found in the anonymous life of Christina of Markyate. This is the story of a holy woman related by an official male biographer.[23] Christina was born into a wealthy family in Huntingdon. While still a child, she visited the abbey of St. Albans and took a secret vow of chastity. In her teens, Ralph Flambard, bishop of Durham, attempted to seduce her. When she resisted he betrothed her to a friend, Burhtred, with the compliance of her parents, the Augustinian prior of Hunting- don, and the bishop of Lincoln. With the support of the archbishop of Canterbury and a hermit called Eadwine, she joined Alwen, a re- cluse at Flamstead, for some two years, and afterward, Roger, a her- mit at Caddington, for four more. At length Abbot Geoffrey of St. Albans build her a convent at Markyate, from which she exercised considerable influence.

Unlike Héloïse, but curiously, rather like Abelard in the *Historia*, Christina does not evolve as a person. Her significance is iconic. She has the same objective throughout the story, which is to pur- sue a chaste, ascetic life, as God intends. The people who change for better or worse are those who come into contact with her— Sueno, Ralph, the bishop of Durham, her father Autti, and the her- mit Roger. It is possible to see a disenchanted Gregorian propagan- dist on behalf of celibacy at work in the caricature of the lecherous Ralph; however, despite the reformist element, the story chiefly en- visages a secular rather than a clerical audience, for whom consen- sual marriage and the attractions of religious communities would be important issues.[24]

No other biography in the period moves so adroitly from the bed- chamber to the monastic cell. Despite the parlor games, Christina's asceticism is intensely intellectual. She differs from figures like Hugh or Guigo in her strongly personal symbolism and in combin- ing radical orality in her devotions with the inspiration of a specific book, the St. Alban's psalter, which appears to have been copied by Roger for her use. Although literate, she deliberately refrains

from writing extensively about herself. This abstinence from literary activity enhances her charisma as a woman, while the official
life written by her male biographer opens her personal history to
an institutional milieu consisting of women and men whom she has
inspired to take up the religious life.

The Life thereby achieves both intimacy and distance. The biographer relates personal details about Christina's emotional misadventures in contrast to his portrayal of her unwavering asceticism.
Yet he does not give evidence of having had any personal conversations with her. In fact, he tells his story in the third person as if it
were the account of a holy woman that had been put together from
both oral and written reports, with the latter acting as source of au-
thentication. This is a standard technique in the period for creating
the impression of literary authority, and one of its purposes is to
permit Christina to establish an archive about herself without engaging directly in literary activity. Her portrait vacillates between
the temptation to master male-dominated scribal institutions, as revealed in her superior understanding of biblical theology, and the
exploiting of the power of unarticulated silence within a community of devoted followers. The rough, untutored Latin style of the
narrative, which occasionally reads like a translation from the vernacular, contrasts with her learnedness, which echoes the gospels,
the uncompromising late Augustine, and, among earlier Lives that
were embellished as religious *romans,* the martyrdom of Alexis.

Less austere disciplinarians turned to Hugh of St. Victor's easy
steps to meditative experience—*lectio, meditatio, oratio, operatio,* and
contemplatio.[25] Few twelfth-century authors applied his scheme literally, but its central elements recur in a variety of arrangements.
The common point of departure is the linking of *lectio* and *meditatio* within a monastic program of "divine reading." This is above all
a community effort: indeed, through the spiritualizing of the text
it is the creation of a textual community, that is, a group of people
whose behavior is in part organized by the common understanding of a set of written directives. This type of social organization, although overlooked by Max Weber, is an example of what he termed
"innerworldly asceticism": it is an active involvement with spiritual
matters that operates rationally, consistently, and in a vocational
fashion in the world, as contrasted with mystical influences that ori-
ent the subject toward withdrawal, renunciation, and the adoption

of an otherworldly lifestyle. The text of the Bible, which is the basis of such innerworldly reflections within a community, is physical, tangible, and perceptible through the senses of hearing and sight. A parallel is furnished by the literary or historical sense within the three- or fourfold scheme of interpretation of the Bible. Beginning in the world, and retaining the link with the world through what is remembered or memorized, the written text rather than abstract ideas is the force that brings together the Augustinian notion of narrative, the twelfth-century emphasis on intentions, and the later medieval and early modern representation of the self through writing, as this genre gradually supersedes the devotional tradition of reading and gives rise to the writing of secular autobiographies.

In this sense, the meditative writers opened a door through which they would have been unwilling to pass. Francis of Assisi, who consolidated their views early in the following century, instinctively understood their dilemma. If they alienated themselves from the literary experience of the Bible, they were unable to say anything meaningful about themselves. On the other hand, if they produced purely literary lives as a result of their biblical studies, they described the self as something other than what it was. The vitality of the self was thereby reduced to a lifeless literary monument. Accordingly, Francis wrote little or nothing about himself, leaving the task to official and unofficial chroniclers who offered contrasting interpretations of his life and thought in response to two different groups of implied readers—one, orthodox, in the Order, the other, heterodox, among the "spirituals."

The two positions on the question of literary experience, for and against writing, are illustrations of opposed interpretations of the same life. There is no precedent for this approach to self-representation in the synoptic gospels, on which Francis's notion of *imitatio* was based, or in earlier saints whose lives were retold by others, for example, by Gérard le Gros for the greatest figure in the previous century's spirituality, Bernard of Clairvaux. In the unofficial story, moreover, the resistance to writing is an attempt to transform biography into what can be described as a type of autobiography. This is accomplished through an adaptation of the notion of imitation in which the readers, instead of following the official published life of the saint, are invited into the intimate circle of "the three friends," where they encounter an alternative that is largely based on oral, unpublished narratives that have been passed from one person to another. In this version of his life, it is empathy rather than texts that is the means of realizing the Franciscan notion of *imitatio.*

The Lives of Francis reveal an implicit understanding of another problem in the field of self-representation that is characteristic of late medieval authors. This is the potential threat to an aspect of faith posed by the twin developments of intentionality and the independent notion of the self. With the direct sustaining role of the deity weakened, it is a short step to construing the self in terms of forces within the individual alone; indeed, to the credibility of self-sustaining "characters," whose psychological portraiture by means of literary description fills the pages of Dante, Boccaccio, and Chaucer. Francis's popularity results from his (perhaps unselfconscious) embracing of a more interdependent view of man and nature than is supported by the philosophy and theology of the thirteenth century, given the primacy of reason in the renascent Aristotelian tradition. Avoiding systematics, just as his twelfth-century predecessors in spirituality had taken exception to the reductive aspects of literary experience, he was able to incorporate naturalistic and subjective concerns into a mystical outlook that stressed the oneness of the individual with his or her surroundings.

As a pillar of this type of spirituality, he is an unlikely candidate for inspiring autobiographies, which become increasingly individualistic after the turn of the thirteenth century. Petrarch's *Secretum,* to which I turn in the next chapter, announces a change in emphasis without, I would argue, necessarily committing its author to the consequences. His correspondence, which he edited and re-edited several times for posterity, confirms the suspicion aroused in the dialogue that, with sacred ontologies weakened, his self is supported by a literary scaffolding whose increasing sophistication camouflages its lack of a convincing theological authority. In the following centuries the contrast between writing and nonwriting recurs in Montaigne and Descartes, the one absorbed by literary tradition, the other apparently rejecting it in favor of a purely conceptual rationality. Montaigne reasserts the ancient view that nothing of permanence can arise through the literary experience of the self, while Descartes, who is essentially in agreement on this point, argues that notions of the self must be grounded in reason alone.

*   *   *

In summary, I would argue that within the problematics of reading, writing, and selfhood we have a phenomenon of *la longue durée* in Western intellectual history.

From the late ancient period, the self is conceived as a potential author whose attitude toward reading and writing helps to determine the type of authority that he or she seeks to impose on a putative audience. If the subject chooses not to engage in reading or writing, literary authority remains oral, personal, and charismatic. Examples include Anthony and Francis at either end of the time frame, both of whom achieve self-definition without resorting to extensive writing, and, in Anthony's case, without much reading either. By contrast, if literate disciplines are involved, authority is transferred to a text that is routinely communicated to its audience through listening, reading, or viewing. One example of this approach is the hermeneutic fashioning of the self by Hugh of St. Victor. Another is Petrarch.

By these twin routes, the ancient spiritual exercise is transformed into the first person meditation by the self-conscious reader or writer. The ancient concern with therapies of the spoken word is reborn as a textual experience in which spiritual healing is a by-product of a process of interpretation. In this approach, the author attempts to create personal well-being through deliberations that imply the presence of readers and writers. *Otium* is reconceived as the reader's leisure, and in the process the words of the written text are frequently the subject of ruminations in which they reacquire the oral immediacy that they had in earlier literary genres like the classical dialogue. In these subtle transitions, the question of identity becomes part of an attempt to communicate thoughts and emotions in order to elicit an ethical judgment in the reader. The reader in turn is conceived as "other," and as a result alienation attains a legitimate status that it does not have in Plotinus or Augustine, the late ancient sources of medieval notions of the *regio dissimilitudinis*. Medieval authors even flirt with the ancient view, championed by Ovid among others, that alienation is a part of the aesthetic evaluation of the literary production by its audience.

During the twelfth century, the power of the divine over individuals' lives is constrained in two ways—by means of human intentions and natural laws. Intentions acquire the capacity to perpetuate autonomous representations of the self in the same way that natural laws are thought to maintain the harmonious operation of the universe. The authority for making statements about the self is thereby transferred in part from the divine to the human sphere, where its twin contexts are discourse and naturalism. In some authors, such as Bernard Silvester and Alan of Lille, discourse and naturalism are combined, while in others, such as Hugh of St. Victor, the intermediary between the outer and inner self is a single meditative literary experience. In all cases, however, a price is paid: the inevitable detaching of the conception of the self from its realistic underpinnings, where Augustine had it firmly anchored. The negative side of this development is the late medieval and early modern author's inability to connect the inner nature of the self with its outer literary expression in a convincing manner, as well as the incapacity to portray inwardness without play, irony, theatrics, or philosophical ambiguity. The question is not whether this transition took place in reality or just in words, as Augustine might have asked, but whether representations of the self in literature ever fully recovered from it.

Chapter Five

Petrarch's Portrait of Augustine

The development of textually oriented contemplative practices in late antiquity and the Middle Ages meant that the activity of the reader was perceived as a technique for achieving a classical philosophical ideal, the betterment of the person. In this respect, reading was for many centuries looked upon as a means to an end rather than an end in itself, even if it was granted that the reader could derive information, edification, or pleasure from an engagement with the text. Petrarch made a contribution to this way of thinking during the period at the end of the Middle Ages when by no means all authors still entertained the view that reading was principally a method for attaining a contemplative state of mind. In the *Secretum* he described relations between reading, writing, and the self in considerable detail, and in the revisions of his correspondence he took pains to present a portrait of himself as a person involved in the otherworldly aspects of literary activity. However, it has proven difficult for scholars to judge the ethical value of this endeavor. One way of approaching the issue is through his recreation of the historical Augustine, whose *Confessions* he read carefully, if somewhat selectively, on the topic of literary values.

By the mid-fourteenth century, when Petrarch conceived his dialogue with the bishop of Hippo, concern with ethics and literature already had a long history.[1] So did attitudes toward reading and writing as methods for acquiring self-knowledge. The chronological boundaries of this discussion can be illustrated through a pair of quotations. The first is from Augustine himself; it is a brief elliptical comment from *De Utilitate Credendi* 7.17: "Cum legerem, per me ipse cognovi. Itane est?" (When I read, it was I who acquired knowledge through myself. Or was it?).[2] This rhetorical question

forms part of Augustine's extensive critique of his reading of classical Latin poetry, especially Virgil, as a student in Madaura and
later in Carthage. He proposes that nothing is learned through the
act of reading itself, just as in *De Magistro*, written two years previously, he maintains that knowledge about realities cannot be acquired uniquely through spoken words. In both cases, we do not
gain information about things through linguistic signs, but through
a type of interior instruction whose origins can be traced ultimately
to God. This means that what one learns when one reads is in some
sense what one knows beforehand, although that knowledge may
not exist in one's conscious thoughts. A decade later, when he wrote
the *Confessions*, Augustine spoke in a similar manner about the problem of self-knowledge. Just as we need to know something beforehand in order to read a text correctly, so there has to be some advance knowledge that permits us to read ourselves correctly. The
understanding that accompanies the reading of a text is derived not
only from the visual perception of graphic signs, but also from the
recognition of what is already in our minds, which is made accessible through an Augustinian adaptation of Platonic reminiscence.
Basing his views on these doctrines, Augustine concluded that the
soul can be educated through reading, but what is permanent in
the soul is not derivable from books. His autobiography became a
canonical document in the history of self-understanding insofar as
the figure of the reader was both utilized and transcended.

The second statement, which I suggest as a terminus ad quem, is
one of the best-known rebuttals of naive faith in book learning in
early modern literature. It is found in the narrative of Descartes's
Discours de la méthode, part 1. Descartes was perhaps unaware of the
tribulations of Augustine's education, but he used the same topos
employed by the bishop of Hippo in stating that he was "nourished
on letters" from childhood but nonetheless rejected the standard
classroom experience of his time. He was taught to believe "that
by means [of books] a clear and certain knowledge could be ob-
tained of all that was useful in life." Yet the more time he spent in
schooling, the less he was convinced that this was the case: "I found
myself embarrassed with so many doubts and errors that it seemed
to me that the effort to instruct myself had no effect other than
the increasing discovery of my own ignorance."[3] Descartes echoes
the Socratic method, ancient skepticism, and possibly Augustine's
notion of *docta ignorantia*, which entered early modern theology

through Nicholas of Cusa. However, in contrast to earlier thinkers, to whom truth was revealed in a single book, the Bible, Descartes undertook a formal refutation of the medieval method of establishing valid knowledge by comparing and consolidating different interpretations of texts. His solution to the problem of uncertainty was a return to the view that was prevalent in Greek thought before the rise of the Jewish and Christian notion that truth could be found in scripture. This was to put his trust in the logic of his own thinking rather than in the knowledge that could be acquired through books. As he reminds us toward the end of the quoted statement, he had no interest in traveling to foreign lands by means of what he read: he preferred to stay at home.

These two statements, which were made respectively in 391 and 1637, loosely frame the age of discovery and disillusionment concerning relations between reading, writing, and self-improvement. Augustine stands at the beginning and Descartes at the end of this lengthy period, which extends through late antiquity, the Middle Ages, and the high Renaissance. Augustine was educated through books but converted through grace. The belief that he could prepare himself for this moment through his readings in philosophy and religion was undermined by his personal experience. Descartes tells a different type of story, but he too rejected bookish education and adopted the viewpoint that valid knowledge can only be acquired through a rational type of demonstration that is free of the mediation of texts.

*   *   *

One of the works of Petrarch in which questions concerning reading and writing are extensively documented is the *Secretum,* that is, the *De Secreto Conflictu Curarum Mearum.*[4] This is a dialogue on spiritual edification that he wrote sometime between 1347 and 1353,[5] possibly as a response to the entry of his brother, Gerard, into the Carthusian monastery at Montrieux, near Toulon, in April 1343. The work was not published during Petrarch's lifetime, but was discovered in Padua in 1378 by Tedaldo della Casa, a Franciscan literary custodian from Santa Croce, Florence. In a marginal note on folio 208 of this codex, written in 1358, Petrarch called the work his intimate reflections (*secreta*), composed "for the peace of his soul, if peace could be found anywhere."[6]

In the preface, Petrarch is visited by an allegorical configuration of Truth. His model for this apparition is *The Consolation of Philosophy*, book 1, prose 1, where the allegorical figure of Philosophy appears before the condemned Boethius, who is silently "turning over" the verses of meter 1 "in his head," before "sealing them through the service of his pen."[7] Important in this opening sentence is the phrase "*tacitus . . . reputarem*," which refers to mental writing and rereading in advance of committing thoughts to the permanent record on parchment, which becomes a second realm of silence. Boethius's cell represents the imprisonment of the soul, which is a neoplatonic commonplace. What is new in his thinking is the suggestion that he can write his way to freedom, or at least ascend through literary activity rather than through a purely spiritual elevation. In keeping with the Platonic hierarchy of the senses, the eye supersedes the ear as Philosophia appears before him in a striking visual image, driving out of his thoughts the aural memory of his sonorous, youthful verses, which provide him with a musical symbol of his former freedom (m.1.1–2):

Carmina qui quondam studio florente peregi,
Flebilis heu maestos cogor inire modos

(I who not so long ago,
when my studies were in flower,
brought poems to completion,
now alas in tears am compelled
to begin again in measures of sadness.)

In his opening statement, Petrarch says that he is astonished as often as he reflects on the manner in which we enter and leave this life: "Attonito michi quidem et sepissime cogitanti qualiter in hanc vitam intrassem, qualiterve forem egressurus" (22). The second part of this sentence recalls *Moral Epistles* 22.14–17,[8] where Seneca, referring to Epicurus, states that wisdom is necessary if a life is to be ended more virtuously than it began. The first part of the sentence, in which Petrarch's phrase "attonito michi . . . cogitanti" parallels the rhythm of Boethius's "mecum tacitus ipse reputarem," introduces still another source. This is Virgil, whose apostrophe to Venus (*O quam te memorem, virgo?*)[9] is quoted as a description of Truth. In contrast to Boethius, for whom Philosophy represents the search for truth, she represents truth itself, which is the goal of philosophical inquiry. In this role she reminds Franciscus (and us) of the excellence of Petrarch's Latin epic, *Africa*, a work not yet completed, and therefore unappreciated, in contrast to his Italian lyrics, which are the "trifles" on which his fame rests. In these plague years, which claimed Laura in 1348, Petrarch's thoughts are evidently less focused on entering a life of philosophy than on finding a philosophically satisfactory manner of leaving this life. At the same time, he adapts the view of life as a preparation for death to his worldly concerns. In dialogue 3, this concern will be expressed as a rationale for literary activity, that is, for the writing of *Africa*.

As we proceed beyond the *Secretum*'s opening lines, the Boethian/Virgilian allegory fades from view, and a Ciceronian/Augustinian dialogue takes shape. This is a conversation whose nearest neighbors are not in the ancient world but in the Middle Ages, for instance, in Dante's discourses with historical figures in the *Commedia*, or in Petrarch's frequent shifts from his past to his present self in the *Canzoniere*.

In ancient dialogues participants normally represent pre-established intellectual positions which the author summarizes through their speeches. These positions are sometimes derived from earlier sources, thereby giving the debate a historical flavor, but the discussion takes place in the present and the arguments are proposed as if they arose from reasoning alone. In the *Secretum*, the words of the interlocutors are spoken in the same time frame, but the dialogue's meaning arises from a sustained historical contrast, since Franciscus is represented as a person in the present while Augustinus is a figure from the distant past. The distinctiveness of the participants arises from their respective locations in historical time rather than from their statements on moral issues.[10] On these matters, their disagreements are sometimes rhetorical. This is clear from dialogue 3, in which their opposed views are presented in a manner that moves toward a synthesis that is completed by the reader. It can even be argued that Petrarch, as the source of the two positions, intended the speakers to represent different sides of a divided personality (just as in his love poetry contrasting emotions form parts of one affective experience). The *Secretum* can thus be viewed as a transformation of Augustine's narrative technique in the *Confessions*, inasmuch as the person Petrarch was (Franciscus) and the person he would like to

be (Augustinus) are configurations of the same character. The fictive dating of the work in 1342, as Guido Martellotti noted, marks
the beginning of the idealistic autobiography Petrarch created both
for his readers and for himself.[11]

This view is confirmed if we look closely at the portrait of Augustine.[12] He is not described as a forceful, eloquent, and engaged
bishop, but as an aged, reflective, and venerable monk.[13] He is dis-
sociated from time, place, and historical circumstances: he is recognized only by generalized qualities, his pious appearance, modest
profile, serious regard, and sober gait.[14] Just before he makes his appearance, Franciscus looks about to see whether Truth is in anyone's
company, or whether she has penetrated his solitude alone.[15] When
Augustine enters the scene, Truth turns from Petrarch toward the
bishop, asking him to break his silent meditation (*taciturna meditatio,
silentium*) with healing words that can be directed toward the poet.
Petrarch magnifies the meditative aspects of the character of the
historical bishop in order to represent his own frustrated desire for
the contemplative life. He accomplishes this task in part by offering
his readers a view of Augustine that was popular among medieval
authors, in particular during the revival of monastic thought after
1050, when the contemplative dimensions of Augustine's sermons
and commentaries were the subject of extensive discussion. This de-
piction of the bishop of Hippo is an indication that the *Secretum* and
the description of the ascent of Mt. Ventoux reflect an interpretive
reading of the *Confessions*.

The historical Augustine, in seeking inner truth, was ambivalent
about book learning, which he associated with the outer arts of language. In its negative dimension, his evaluation of the reading process recalls the suspicions of the desert fathers, and has more in
common with the skepticism of Montaigne than with the uncom-
plicated enthusiasm for rediscovered classics that was inaugurated
by the humanism of Petrarch. For Augustine, reading is a means
of education, but there is no spiritual transformation *sola scriptura,*
to use Luther's celebrated phrase. Petrarch uses Augustine's ideas
about reading as a point of departure in the *Secretum*, but he more
readily accepts the idea that reading and spiritual progress can be
harmoniously united in a person who embarks on a philosophical
journey through life.[16] Trudging up Mt. Ventoux in 1336, *Confessions*
in hand,[17] he chiefly senses Augustine's literary presence,[18] whereas
for Augustine, who converted to the religious life in Milan in 386,

the only text actually present, Romans 13:13–14, brought about an instantaneous transcending of the educational experience of the earlier books of the *Confessions*. In Augustine, the change from a secular to a religious outlook is sudden and irrevocable; in Petrarch, the spiritual component is progressively incorporated into a layman's view of the world.[19]

Only through a considerable change from his role in the *Confessions*, therefore, can the historical Augustine be envisaged as the official guide on an intellectual journey whose goal is the production of a book. As a part of this reconfiguration, Petrarch invests the reader with an ethical role that is lacking in the *Confessions*. During the three days of conversation in the *Secretum,* Truth is silent, while Franciscus and Augustinus engage in debate. It is the reader, therefore, through the eyes of Truth, who ultimately passes judgment on his activities as an author. Augustinus and Franciscus engage in a dialogue that is supposed to be directed against the moral evils of the day,[20] but the *Secretum* does not follow the plan consistently, and, as a result the work cannot be considered an early prototype of more overtly satirical writings in this genre, such as Erasmus's *Praise of Folly*. In fact, there is little criticism of established religious institutions even in comparison with Petrarch's other works, such as the *Liber Sine Nomine.* Instead, two important themes in his religious writings make their appearance. He defends the otherworldly values associated with the monastic life and he advances the view that a literary work can criticize secularism while remaining within the secular world, because it is accessible, as a book, to the lay reading public.

We can ask whether this dual message is the work's real secret. If it is, it involves a substitution of Petrarchan for Augustinian goals. Among these, classical reminiscence, which is influential on Augustine's thinking, is replaced by the artificial memory of the text. In Augustine external aids to recall are intended to provide clues to inner recognition. In Petrarch the textual record is autonomous and, like its author, self-referential, which makes it possible, as it is not for Augustine, for the individual to become in some sense his own book. The pair likewise differ in their attitude toward the book's ethical status. While they share the view that oral dialogue should be set down in writing as an act of preservation, Petrarch has a more difficult time than Augustine convincing his readers that he does not have the hidden aim of creating a literary monument. In his words, his purpose is neither to add to his publications nor to seek additional fame through his activities as an author, but simply to reexperience, as a reader of the *Secretum*, the pleasantness that he once enjoyed in conversation.[21] Whereas Augustine uses texts as a means toward attaining a higher end, Petrarch more than occasionally looks on the text, or its mentally recreated meaning, as an end in itself. The final statement in his preface is not directed to Truth or Augustinus but to the book itself, the *libellus* that is described allegorically as it "flees the meetings of men, happy to remain within itself."[22] The interiority Augustine associates with the mind has thus become a type of literary solitude, a recreation of meaning in tranquility, whence, perhaps, Petrarch entitles the written version of his dialogue a *secretum*, that is, something sequestered and hidden away.

Ernest Hatch Wilkins spoke of the *Secretum* as Petrarch's "equivalent of the *Confessions* of St. Augustine."[23] The comparison would have pleased Petrarch. However, in addition to its obvious points of contact with the autobiography, the *Secretum* reflects themes from the dialogues Augustine wrote in the winter and early spring of 386–387, after his reconversion to Catholicism, and from *De Vera Religione*, written in 390–391, which Petrarch quoted at the end of book 1 of the *Secretum* from a copy he himself had annotated.[24] If we except the brief references to *Confessions* 8.7–12 in dialogues 1 and 2 and the indirect echo of the theme of *docta ignorantia* from *Confessions*, book 10, near the beginning of dialogue 2, the Augustinian themes in the *Secretum* can as easily be traced to the early writings as to the autobiography. These include the major subjects of each day, respectively death, the virtues and vices, and sin and penance, as well as the general themes of regret and melancholy.[25] There are important allusions to *The City of God* and traces of influence from the *Retractions*.[26] However, it is in Augustine's early writings that we first see the constellation of late classical sources that reappears in the *Secretum*. The non-Christian author most often cited by Petrarch is Virgil, followed closely by Cicero, Horace, and Seneca. The shared philosophical influence is Cicero's *Tusculan Disputations*. This is the Cicero of Augustine's conversion to philosophy at age nineteen rather than the pagan philosopher whom the bishop of Hippo may have disparaged later in life.[27]

I have spoken of a personal interpretation of the *Confessions*. Petrarch thinks that the work is almost entirely about conflict within the self. This is a modernist view that was created in part, I believe, by Petrarch himself. Other important Augustinian themes are neglected, for instance the discussions of time, memory, the incarnation, and non-Christian philosophies. In the *Secretum*, which attempts to idealize Laura, there is no serious mention of Augustine's model woman, Monica.[28] The main subject of the *Secretum* is Petrarch (although, as noted, his thinking is sometimes represented by Augustinus). By contrast, a silent God, not the author of the written text, is the true hero of the *Confessions*. In the narrative books, Augustine is an actor in a prearranged drama, rather like a Greek tragedy, the meaning of which is not known to him beforehand but is worked out in the course of the presentation.

The two writers differ in their conception of a divided self. In the early books of the *Confessions*, Augustine remains under the lingering influence of Manichaean dualism, which is only overcome through the combined instruction of Ambrose, Plotinus or Porphyry, and Paul. In Petrarch it is not philosophies that cause division in the self but the play of his emotions: the tension between heat and cold, fire and ice, and communion and loneliness by which Franciscus characterizes his attitude toward Laura in the Italian lyric poetry.[29] For Petrarch, these are the emotions of a reader, as Franciscus makes clear when he tells Augustinus: "When I read the books of your *Confessions*, I find myself as often torn between two contrary feelings, hope and fear. My joy is mixed with sadness: for, as I read, I do not think of the story of someone else's errancy, but of my own."[30] Franciscus's emotions arise out of what he reads (*legere* is repeated twice in the quoted sentence); Augustine's do not. A careful study of the *Confessions* in relation to books 1 to 3 of *De Doctrina Christiana*, which were written about the same time, would have taught Petrarch that by 397 Augustine had come to distrust the emotions created by literature. One of the genres he singled out for criticism was epic poetry, which Petrarch was attempting to compose, as his masterpiece to be left to posterity, about the time that he was writing the *Secretum*. What was considered to be inauthentic by Augustine, as a substitution for experience, was through literature a source of authenticity in Petrarch.

*   *   *

The reasons for these differences in attitude can be clarified if we take account of some literary developments in Petrarch's time. In order to put them in perspective, let me return to my point of departure: the suggestion that Augustine and Descartes stand at opposite ends of a lengthy period that sees the development of the theme of the self in the literary activities of reading and writing.

The first phase of this history occurs in antiquity and late antiquity. During this period there are a number of references to reading and writing in discussions of the self; they are not widespread, however, and the preferred manner of talking about the self is simply as an aspect of soul or mind, as it is in ancient and Hellenistic philosophy. The second phase extends roughly from Othloh of St. Emmeram (d. ca. 1070) to Francis of Assisi (d. 1226). During these two centuries there is a rise in the number and variety of discussions of reading, writing, and the self. In general, the statements are in Latin, their authors are largely religious men and women, and the main source is the Bible, together with patristic and hagiographic texts. The third phase extends from the thirteenth to the seventeenth centuries. The statements are in the vernacular languages as well as Latin, the authors are lay and religious men and women, and the themes are taken from both the Bible and classical literature. Petrarch is an innovative figure in this last period, inasmuch as the *Secretum* makes the traditional religious subject of the active and the contemplative life a part of a secular literary career. The classical notion of cultivated leisure is reinstated and pagan and Christian models of the virtuous life are combined.

At the center of this early humanist vision is the notion of solitude. Petrarch believes that a precondition of self-understanding is withdrawal from the world: from the town to the countryside, from the business of life to inward calm and reflectiveness. For the first time since late antiquity, it is the secular library and not the monastic cell that is the image of this solitude.[31] Petrarch's isolation is likewise dissimilar to earlier expressions of the theme of solitude in requiring witnessing by an audience. He is not a hermit: he admits a companion or two, provided that he can retreat into a private, meditative realm, alone, in order to write.[32] But he is not totally isolated, as were ascetics like Anthony in the fourth century or Guigo I in the twelfth: he is in touch with his community, which consists in his present and future readership. His silence is therefore a time of recreation and literary activity.[33] In exhibiting this ambivalence toward the more isolated asceticism of earlier monastic tradition, he effectively modifies Augustine's view of the manner in which the individual can escape from his or her worldly entanglements. In Augustine it is the religious life that permits the individual to be in the world but not of the world; in Petrarch, it is the literary life. The contrast is between a religious and a literary conversion to otherworldly values.

Petrarch introduces the notion of solitude in the *Secretum* by means of a number of ancient sources. In dialogue 2, Augustinus quotes Seneca, *Epistle* 65.21: "I am greater, and was born to greater things, than that I might be the slave of my body."[34] Franciscus reinforces the sentiment with a quotation from *Africa* in which Scipio speaks of the souls that are freed from the body's shackles:

Odimus et laqueos et vincula nota timemus
libertatis onus: quod nunc sumus illud amamus
(*Africa*, 1.329–30)

(We despise the fetters, and we fear the chains
we have known, the burden of the liberty,
which, when we have it, we love.)

By the time we reach dialogue 3, this neoplatonic position is inseparable from Petrarch's conception of authorship as a means of achieving otherworldly goals. In a renowned speech, Augustinus points out that Franciscus owes his talents to the generosity of nature but that his devotion to Laura has prevented him from realizing his potential. "That form seemed to you so pleasant, so sweet, that all that might have been harvested from the seeds of innate virtue has been laid waste—burned in the heat of your desire, flooded in the showers of your tears."[35] And he adds: "Thus, the person whom you spoke of as your guide, while she drew you away from baser desires, has led you into a glittering pit."[36] Petrarch protests that he loves Laura for her soul only: the proof is that the older she is, the greater is his admiration. Augustine is unconvinced by this sophistry. In recalling Petrarch's pangs of love, he introduces another image of solitude, a Homeric couplet describing Bellerophon, the beautiful youth who was abandoned by the gods after his many misadventures. The lines are quoted in Latin from Cicero, *Tusculan Disputations*, 3.26.63:

Qui miser in campis merens errabat alienis
ipse suum cor edens, hominum vestigia vitans.

(He wandered in sadness, miserable,
through alien fields, avoiding the paths of men,
as his heart devoured itself.)

In dialogue 3 Augustinus says that Petrarch should seek solitude
only when his memory of Laura has vanished. Otherwise, he risks
taking his troubles with him wherever he goes to seek the solitary
life.

The inspiration for this complex notion of literary achievement
through spiritual withdrawal is taken from the monastic life and
makes its appearance in works written by Petrarch between 1342
and 1353.[37] These include an early version of the *Secretum*, some
parts of *Rerum Memorandarum Libri*, and the popular *Penitential
Psalms* at the beginning of the decade, as well as parts of *De Vita Solitaria* and *De Otio Religioso*, which were written later. Petrarch did not
entertain the idea of becoming a monk, despite the warm relations
that he enjoyed with a number of religious communities. However,
his recreation of monastic ideals in a literary context in the writings of this period offers a background, perhaps an explanation,
for the combination of religious and secular ideals that make their
appearance in his conception of the self in the *Secretum*. If he is a
spokesman on behalf of the early humanist outlook, he is something of an idealist in his view of the monastic past. He provides his
readers with a synthetic image of the solitary life evidently drawn
from monastic sources; this is contrasted with the worldliness of the
church, secular society, and his own literary efforts. His personal
reconceptualization of the monastic life through literary sources,
and the antimodernism it implies, may be partly responsible for his
shortsighted views on the achievements of his contemporaries in
science, medicine, and systematic philosophy. Above all, through
his conception of literary solitude he reaches the conclusion that
the reading and writing in which he is engaged can be looked on am-
bivalently: positively, as a pathway to inner reflection, or negatively,
as a concentration on outer forms of expression. The life of letters
can thereby become a symbol of the spiritual conflict within himself
that is developed in his dialogue with the historical Augustine.

If the discussion of Laura brings this potential twosidedness into perspective in dialogue 3, it is the presence of Augustinus throughout the *Secretum* that provides the theological context for Petrarch's views. The distance between Augustine and Augustinus is increased by Petrarch's reinstatement of a combination of Christian and classical literary ideals that the bishop of Hippo rejected after 396. Petrarch also abandons Augustine's austere conception of grace in favor of the more moderate teachings of theologians after the twelfth century. His personal interpretation of Augustine, together with his synthetic view of medieval religious life as a development out of Augustine's thought, provides the intellectual context for the discussion of monasticism in the *Secretum*.[38] His characterization of monastic ideas may have been generalized in order to avoid having to deal with the endemic problems of the monastic orders in the fourteenth century; however, it was principally his desire to ground his views in the doctrines of an ancient thinker that led him to focus on Augustine and to omit other figures of historical importance whose spiritual biographies he summarized in *De Vita Solitaria*. He portrays the monastic life in utopian terms as a set of principles for conduct that can presumably be adapted to all times and circumstances.

In this configuration, he envisages that way of life as a type of "otherness": it is a pattern of behavior from which he is alienated, since he does not himself know it in person except through brief experiences. It is perhaps for that reason that he makes Augustinus a rather transparent literary creation. The bishop of Hippo is a bearer of rules of conduct rather than a living person like the Laura of his poetry or the literary representation of himself. If this is Petrarch's intention, we should not look on monasticism as the life he would have preferred, as he occasionally tries to persuade us, and consequently view his literary achievement as a desertion of this religious ideal, as Augustinus suggests. It is equally incorrect to see poetic inspiration overcoming religious sentiments in his characterization of himself, which is another recurring otherworldly theme in the *Secretum*. The two images—the reluctant monk and the dissatisfied *littérateur*—are continually played off against each other in both his poetry and his prose.

It is the ancient rhetoric for framing the question of the active versus the contemplative life that is privileged in the *Secretum*. The chief source is the correspondence of Seneca, whom, ironically, Augustinus is frequently made to quote, although the historical Augustine almost never does so in his own writings. It is here rather than in Augustine that Petrarch found his cherished notion of the embodiment of the self in the ethical dimension of the literary life. In *Moral Epistles* 2, Seneca tells Lucilius that there is no better proof of a well-ordered mind than a person's ability to remain where he is and pass some hours with himself. Seneca's advice to his friend is to cultivate himself through reading but to be discriminating in his choice of authors. When the mind is everywhere, it is nowhere in particular (*Ep.*, 2). If Lucilius cannot read all the books he owns, his mind should be in possession of those he has read (*Ep.*, 2). Furthermore, he should not be continually poring over these volumes or sitting at his writing-desk. His mind has to have some time to itself in order to be brought back to life (*Ep.*, 15). Seneca anticipates Petrarch's view that it is possible for spiritual renewal to take place through an author's style of writing (*Ep.*, 46). It is best to read texts in company, as an extension of friendship, since nothing of value is truly enjoyed unless it is shared with someone else. Accordingly, Seneca sends Lucilius books with useful passages marked, so that he can turn immediately to the statements his mentor admires (*Ep.*, 6). Reading nonetheless imposes on the individual a type of literary solitude that Petrarch will recreate through reading the Latin classics and writing poetry. For both authors, reading and writing are ways of fleeing the masses and their anonymity. Seneca spends his nights with his books; he has little time for sleep. His studies are his form of withdrawal from business and society (*Ep.*, 8). This is the philosophy sought by Petrarch, which molds the character and creates wisdom (*Ep.*, 16).

It was in medieval monastic writings that Petrarch found a model for placing these beliefs within a consistent literary and ascetic program, thereby knitting together the isolated thoughts Montaigne was later to call his "pièces décousues." The ideal of earlier monastic thinking, whose goal was to escape from the subjectivity of the self, became part of a literary endeavor whose goal was to keep that subjectivity firmly within the reader's view. As a consequence, in Petrarch's transformation of the monastic outlook the self no longer resonates with its own inwardness, but with the inward meaning of texts that are read, written, or mentally recreated. Among Petrarch's sources for his literary interpretation of monasticism may have been

Bernard of Clairvaux, William of St. Thierry, Aelred of Rievaulx, and the Victorines.[39] He may have drawn on the notion of active leisure in prayer, liturgy, or divine reading as it was represented by the Dominicans and the Franciscans.[40] He could have discussed monastic themes with his friends in religious communities, among them the learned Dionigi da Borgo San Sepolcro, the commentator of Valerius Maximus, who gave him his precious manuscript of the *Confessions.*

Petrarch's piety is no less genuine because it is expressed in the style and content of an earlier period's spirituality. Yet the gulf between him and earlier monastic authors was unbridgeable, as he knew. His writings on the theme of the contemplative life were as popular with contemporary readers as his lyric poetry. Apart from the *Canzoniere*, their favorite books were the *Secretum*, the *Penitential Psalms*, *De Vita Solitaria*, and *De Remediis.* These works enabled his secular readers to participate in a way of thinking that was no longer a part of their everyday knowledge, and to do so largely through literature. They participated in a brief revival of medievalism in fourteenth-century Italy and France that was possibly a reaction to hard times, rampant disease, republican strife, and ecclesiastical abuse. Petrarch was closer to the realities of monastic life than many of his readers, and he appears to have been reluctant to accept the finality of the historical distance that he himself helped to create. In detaching the representation of the inner life from the subjective understanding of that life, as he attempted to do in the *Secretum*, he therefore spoke on behalf of a broad conflict that was developing in European letters over the legitimacy of any literary configuration of the self. In that, perhaps, he was at his most modern.

Chapter Six

Two Versions of Utopia

The century that has just finished has been greatly troubled by utopian schemes. Some of these projects have doubtless been a source of social progress, especially in the less developed world, but even their enthusiastic supporters would agree that the cost in human lives has been unacceptably high. As a consequence, most of us nowadays would be skeptical, if not openly hostile, toward global blueprints for changing society. At best, they would be viewed satirically as "dystopias," as they were by Samuel Butler, George Orwell, and Aldous Huxley.

Serious interest in utopian thinking goes back to Plato's *Republic*, as well as to statements about ideal commonwealths in Cicero, Seneca, Marcus Aurelius, and Plotinus, who dreamed of founding a philosopher's village south of Rome called Platonopolis. After Plato, it is Augustine who offers the most extensive reflections on the subject in antiquity. Unlike Plato, who took up the issues in abstract terms, Augustine gave consideration to societies that actually existed. He was notable for believing in the possibility of achieving a perfect community, at least for those who were fortunate enough to be elected into it, and he called this the eternal or heavenly city. As a consequence, he rejected the claims of the two main candidates for the status of eternal cities in his time, Jerusalem and Rome. In his opinion, Jerusalem was eternal only in a prophetic sense, while Rome had forfeited its claim to perpetuity on moral grounds long before the city was overrun by the Visigoths under Alaric on 24 August 410.

Like Plato, Augustine preferred to think of the utopian or eternal city chiefly as a problem in philosophy. The critical question was the relationship of the city's alleged eternity to the inevitable passage of time. If this were truly the best sort of society, it would presumably contain within itself the conditions of its own perpetuation, as an aspect of this perfection. How could this state of affairs be achieved among human societies, which were clearly impermanent?

The work in which Augustine addressed these problems at length is *The City of God*, which was written in stages between 412 and 427. In the first part of this chapter I discuss what he says on these topics in a programmatic statement he made in the middle of this work, when he had finished his analysis of the earthly city and was beginning to talk about the heavenly city. I comment briefly on his interpretation of the writings of Plotinus, since it was through them that he arrived at a historical understanding of an ideal city that differed from the ahistorical commonwealth in Plato's *Republic*.

In the second part of the chapter I turn to an author who read both Plato and Augustine but who adopted an original approach to the same topic. This is Thomas More, whose *Utopia* was published in 1516. William Roper, More's son-in-law and biographer, tells us that More gave a public reading of *The City of God* in St. Lawrence's church, London, in 1501, when he was twenty-three. We do not know what More said, but Thomas Stapleton, another of More's biographers, notes that Augustine was approached "not from the theological point of view, but from the standpoint of history and philosophy."[1] Nicolas Harpsfield recalls that the audience included the vicar of St. Lawrence, William Grocyn,[2] who may have been teaching More the rudiments of Greek that he himself had acquired a few years earlier in Italy. More was thereby enabled to read Plato in the original, whereas Augustine only knew the *Republic* through the translation of Cicero.

There is no doubt that Augustine was a serious influence on More's outlook. However, the debt is more noticeable in the devotional writings than in *Utopia*. In the latter work the ancient author most often mentioned is Plato. In the verses that were prefixed to the 1516 and 1518 editions, More speaks of his island kingdom, not altogether modestly, as rivaling, even surpassing, Plato's republic.[3] One of the questions that has remained unanswered in research on More is what this statement means. More may have thought that the institutions of Utopia were superior to those of the *Republic* because they portrayed a living rather than an imaginary society.[4] On the other hand, the alleged superiority may have arisen from More's conviction that all utopian projects are futile, since the genetic faults in human societies cannot be corrected merely by changing the institutions by which they are maintained over time. In this case, his position would have been similar to that of Augustine, who believed that societies are improvable but that their inherent limitations can never fully be overcome.

*   *   *

I believe that More shared Augustine's pessimism on this aspect of utopian thinking, but the work that he produced by way of illustration is very different from *The City of God*. It is therefore legitimate to ask what, if anything, he may have found useful in Augustine in working out his distinctively humanist perspective on the problem of society's betterment.[5]

The point of departure for such an inquiry is Augustine's understanding of the connection between societies in the existing world and those of the imagination. A related issue is the nature of the timelessness that he envisaged in an ideal society. Finally, an explanation has to be found for his belief, in contrast to Plato and More, that our reflections on utopian projects are usually based on the authority of inherited beliefs rather than on pure reason.

Augustine tackled the first of these questions in a bold statement at the beginning of book 11 of *The City of God*[6] where he says that "the two cities, the earthly and the heavenly, [are] interwoven (*perplexas*), as it were, in this present transitory world, and intermingled (*permixtas*) with each other."[7]

In the next paragraph he provided his readers with a commentary in which he explained this connection and briefly summarized the salient points of his theology presented in the previous ten books. His explanation takes the form of describing an experience and subsequently specifying its function in utopian thinking. He first says that it is a momentous and somewhat rare occurrence for someone who has reflected on the created universe, in both its corporeal and incorporeal dimensions, to be able to achieve meditative withdrawal through the concentration of the mind. He then mentions two intellectual benefits that accrue from this mental retirement. The individual comes nearer to the changeless substance of God and learns through this proximity that everything in the universe apart from himself has been made by God and by God alone.[8]

In a single lengthy sentence that effectively introduces books 11 to 22, Augustine thus envisages the Christian philosopher, who is of course himself, in a moment of meditation on God and the universe. In the first instance, therefore, we can say that in his view the earthly and heavenly cities are commingled in the present by the manner in which we think about them. The conception that modern thought calls "utopia" is nothing more or less than the result of the reflections that arise from this "attention" or "intention" of the mind (*intentione mentis*). During this period of contemplation we entertain an image, or, as some would say, an illusion, of the timelessness of a utopian society. While we engage in this meditative exercise, we are nonetheless aware that we are thinking about something that is the product of our imagination rather than of our experience in the world. In the end we cannot know what a truly timeless world is like, since our minds, as they engage in this type of thought, are not timeless but the product of temporal flow.

Augustine's statement on this question can be compared to the better-known discussion of the meaning of time in *Confessions* 11. There, as noted, he solves the problem of time through a reading aloud of the first line of Ambrose's hymn, *Deus creator omnium*. It is through the memory of the syllables, after the sound of the spoken words has ceased, that we arrive at the meaning of the hymn's initial phrase.[9] In *The City of God* he presents a different but parallel account of the same phenomenon. He asks us what it would be like if we did not think in words, which, when spoken, provide an image of the passage of time, but in concepts which, as they exist in our thoughts, appear to be independent of the temporal dimension. Furthermore, he inquires into what sort of language this would be,[10] and how we would communicate with a being that was capable of speaking it. His conclusion is that this language of thought would have to be translated into words if we were to be able to understand it. Again, the nontemporal would become temporal.

A being that could communicate in this fashion would presumably be not human but divine. Moreover, if divinity is so defined, this being would have to be a single God rather than a pantheon of gods, since its ability to convey meaning could not vary with respect to specific human languages.[11] In other words, if there is a language of thought, it has to be a conceptualized language, although it can be translated into many spoken languages. It follows that this mental language does not have to impart its meaning through sounds that reverberate in the atmosphere, or by means of dreams, visions, or other mental phenomena in which something comparable to communication through words takes place.[12] These are merely avenues for interchange that have been invented so that humans, who are incapable of understanding thought by means of thought, can do so by means of words. Is it possible in some circumstances for this conceptualized language to enter directly into our thoughts, informing us concerning realities, that is, concerning things as they always are? Yes, but in order to comprehend statements by means of this type of discourse, we would have to learn to hear with the mind rather than with the body (*ad audiendum mente, non corpore*, 11.2). This is the purpose of our withdrawal from the senses and from the passage of time through mental concentration.

There are thus two initial steps in our understanding of the connection between the temporal and the eternal: first, withdrawal from the senses to the mind, where we discover the nontemporal mode, and secondly, recognition that our awareness of the nontemporal mode does not arise from the passage of time, at least as this is measured by speech.

The third stage has to do with the limits of our reasoning capacities and experiential knowledge. Augustine has established that through observation and experiment we can learn how to measure the passage of time. We can therefore conclude that there is a difference between time and eternity. However, by this process of reasoning we do not discover what eternity is but only what it is not, since the same logic by which we measure time tells us that we are unable to measure non-time. We seem to be able to understand eternity in relation to time, but we cannot understand eternity in relation to itself.

Trying to understand the timeless is like trying to understand the nature of any type of existence, including our own. We know *that* we exist: Augustine proves the point through the argument of the *cogito*.[13] But knowing that we exist in a subjective sense, like being aware of the passage of time, does not tell us anything about the transcendent nature of existence, as Husserl remarked in an Augustinian moment in his *Cartesian Meditations*.[14] In attempting to grasp the meaning of such notions, we have to recognize the limits of our experiential understanding of the world. When we reach this frontier we are reduced to assertions based on trust or faith: these affirm that something is the case, but there is no proof (or disproof) for what is said. We are dealing with beliefs, assumptions, or probabilities rather than facts.

If the knowledge of the eternal manages to get into our minds, as it evidently does, and its source is not time as we know it, then we have to account for the way the information make its way to its destination. Augustine proposes that this transition is accountable to the presence of the deity in us. We are made in the "image and likeness of God" to the degree that we are capable of understanding concepts like eternity that have their origin in him. As mortals we are created and pass away, but through God's trace in us we participate in immortality, in part through the mental recreation of meaning. We all possess this vestige of the eternal, through which we realize, or, as Augustine would say, recall, the eternal quality of the heavenly city while living on earth.

Making God the source of timelessness is not an adequate solution to the problem, since we do not have a direct experience of God any more than we do of non-time. The philosophical question is why we believe that such knowledge, which is not based on observation or experience, is dependable. Augustine's position, as stated in the *Confessions*, is that we believe in all sorts of things that we cannot personally verify. For example, we learn who our parents are from the reports of others, since we are not fully conscious at the time of our birth. We believe that these statements are accurate, just as we make assumptions concerning other sources of continuity in our lives. Our personal narratives are constructed from a tissue of such beliefs. In this sense, our self-understanding is an interpretive experience based on a combination of reason and faith.

Augustine thus establishes that we have a notion of the eternal that is not the product of our knowledge of the world in which we live. He also argues that this knowledge is superior to our understanding of time, since in eternity things are as they always are, whereas, in our experience, things exist impermanently, owing to the passage of time. Yet the mind, which evidently has the capacity to rise to the eternal through an act of will, seldom does so, and, when it does, the eternal does not appear to hold our attention for long before our thoughts return to temporal matters. Why is this so?

Augustine provides one answer in the vision at Ostia in *Confessions*, book 9. A few days before Monica's death, he and his mother had a momentary vision of the paradise of the elect. Their conversation passed from words to silence, and for a few moments they enjoyed the perfect communication of minds to which Augustine refers in his description of the conditions for the eternal in *The City of God*, 11.2. When he returns to the theme in the later work, he does not speak about his personal history but about the human condition in general. Also, a greater emphasis is placed on the negative implications of meditative experience. He proposes that the human mind has an innate capacity for reason, but that its potential for virtuous action has been reduced through the habitual practice of vice. As a result, the mind is not capable of the direct perception of truth, just as the eyes are not able to gaze directly at a bright light. Having deserted truth, the mind has to be led back, step by step, and, as it has lost its way, it needs a trustworthy guide. In Augustine's view, this is the meaning of the gospel narrative in which truth appeared on earth in the form of eternity's offspring by means of the incarnation. In this story, the eternal became temporal and the temporal was for a time eternal.

The theology of this statement is familiar enough to require little commentary. Let us note, however, that Augustine has effectively changed the direction of his thinking in accounting for the interdependence of time and eternity in the concept of the two cities. In the first part of his explanation he is concerned with the philosophy of language. His major initiative has to do with communication in words and in thoughts. In the second part he is chiefly concerned with establishing a narrative theology. The change can be illustrated by the way in which he describes God and Christ. In the first section of the discussion, God is termed an unchanging substance (*incommutabilis substantia*); in the second, Christ is called the mediator (*mediator*) in parallel with the concepts of mankind (*homo*) and the way (*uia*). He states, "For through this he was the mediator, through this a man, and through this the way,"[15] in imitation of the commentary on the biblical narrative at 1 Tim. 2:5: "Unus est Deus, unus et mediator Dei et hominum, homo Christus Jesus."

In this move from language philosophy to narrative theology an important role is played by Augustine's transformation of Plotinus's notion of our relationship to the eternal. In his reworking of a Platonic expression, Plotinus compares the eternal to a homeland from which we have been separated as a metaphorical way of describing how the one became the many. Augustine translates this notion of estrangement or alienation by the phrase *regio dissimilitudinis* (the region of unlikeness), an expression, as noted, that has a lengthy subsequent history in thinking about utopia down to the modern concept of social alienation.[16] Like Plotinus, Augustine suggests that there is a way for us to return to our homeland (*patria*), but, in contrast to his mentor, he argues that this journey takes us beyond what can be accomplished by a personal mental ascent through meditation. In his view, "homecoming" is a metaphor that describes our relationship to time and history and is thereby a part of the cosmic process that created human societies and determines their inevitable decline. In this sense, Augustine is a type of historicist.

There is one further stage in Augustine's explanation of time and eternity in this introductory statement, which is presented in 11.3. If the first step concerns words and thoughts and the second discusses a living narrative, this part of the argument involves the written word of scripture.

His thinking can be explained if we return to the notion that in everyday life there is a hierarchy of types of evidence on which we base beliefs about the continuity of our personal narratives. By extension, we can say that we put reliable authority above hearsay evidence, and (in general) we give greater credibility to written than to oral accounts of events because we can refer to them when checking facts. This hierarchy helps us make judgments in our personal lives, and by analogy it provides us with a method for judging statements in other accounts, including those in sacred texts. When Christ spoke (in the gospel narratives) his words were uttered in a tradition of oral discourse that was preceded by the Jewish prophets and followed by the Christian apostles. By contrast, after the end of the apostolic age, he had to speak to us by means of the canonical scriptures, which comprise the authenticated transcript of his life and thought. Augustine did not know that the texts of the gospel were transmitted orally before they were written down, but he recognized that these writings relate oral discourses he and his contemporaries could not have heard for themselves. In addition to believing that the gospel accounts are revealed truth,[17] Augustine thus proposed the original view that we accept the transcript of these words on authority. It is through this written authority that such statements replace the actual words of Christ as the source of our spiritual direction.

This is a development of Augustine's argument concerning our trust, faith, or belief in things we cannot know. We acquire knowledge of things that are present through our external or internal senses, and the knowledge of things that are not present through the reports of others. If we can learn about visible things in these ways, we can also learn about invisible things, which are known through the mind or soul.[18] The written text of the Bible can replace the direct communication of God, which, he noted, "magnum est et admodum rarum,"[19] even for those who have this experience in a moment of mystical elevation. In everyday life it is through reading the Bible that we achieve a meditative state of mind, and as a consequence it is through reflecting on the Bible's message that we find our way to the utopian concept of the city of God.

*   *   *

There is a great deal more that can be said about Augustine's concepts of time and eternity in *The City of God*. Let me remind the reader that I have been talking about just three ideas that are developed in the opening chapters of book 11. These concern the connection between the temporal and the eternal cities, the role of meditation in understanding this connection, and the reading of the Bible as a point of departure for the process of reflection, which Augustine extends in books 11 to 22.

Thomas More's *Utopia* begins with rather different priorities. Let us return to the verses that were prefixed to the 1516 and 1518 editions (quoted above, note 3): "I was called No Place by the ancients, owing to my isolation; but now I am the rival of Plato's republic, perhaps even its victorious successor, for what he described in words, I myself have presented through men, potential works, and outstanding laws: rightly I should be called by the name of Happy Place." In these lines there are effectively two speaking voices, the island of Utopia and Thomas More. It is Utopia who is *ego* (in line 3), but Utopia expresses what are in fact More's sentiments, since it is he who has made the island less isolated (*infrequentia*) by telling the world about it.

Utopia thus begins with an assertion of the view shared by More and Erasmus on the potential role of books and print culture in relieving the civic and moral ignorance of mankind. This statement is followed by More's boast that Utopia is superior to Plato's republic: the project is presented as a literary work (*literis*), and offers his readers as well a description of a real society in which they can appreciate what has been accomplished by men, resources, and excellent laws (*viris & opibus, optimisque legibus*). Accordingly, *Utopia*, book 2, consists of a detailed description of Utopia's institutions. While Plato spends much of the *Republic* telling us about the guardians' training program, book 2 is envisaged as a practical set of proposals in which More corrects abuses on such matters as political tyranny, the use of mercenaries, and the evils of the enclosure movement.

Two of More's principal reasons for writing *Utopia* are thus stated in these verses: his belief in the value of education as an aspect of religious reform, and his criticism of the social and political evils of contemporary England. He raises a third issue in his play on *utopia* and *eutopia* (no place and happy place).[20] This type of wordplay has both a satirical function, which is evident in the "barbaric" Latin words with Greek roots that are employed for types of people and their roles in *Utopia*,[21] and a serious function, which is to allude to a traditional Christian theme that is taken up by Augustine in numerous works written between *On the Happy Life* and *The City of God.* This is the view that there is a happy place where life does not end, but, because humans live and die in time, it is not a place they know. As a result, for humans *eutopia*, the happy place, is literally *utopia*, no place.

There is no evidence that More took this idea directly from Augustine. In any case, there was no need for him to do so, since it was a commonplace in the literature of *contemptus mundi* with which he was familiar after spending three years in the Charterhouse in London. The same can be said for another idea More appears to have assimilated from earlier sources: his belief in the limits of human rationality. Like Plato's *Republic* and *Laws*, Utopia is designed as a society based on reason alone. As R. W. Chambers pointed out in a classic study,[22] Utopia is thereby limited in the Christian view to the perfection of the four cardinal virtues, wisdom, fortitude, temperance, and justice, while it lacks the three Christian virtues, faith, hope, and charity,[23] which presumably have to be imported by missionaries. In this respect More follows a well-established tradition of thinking about pagan notions of civic life during the Middle Ages, which is illustrated by works as different as Dante's *Commedia* and *Piers Plowman*. More's innovation in this tradition is to make his philosophers into educated non-Europeans in order to satirize the cultural shortcomings of his countrymen.

It is now widely acknowledged that Chambers's outstanding study of *Utopia* has the weakness of placing rather too great an emphasis on the medieval aspects of *Utopia* such as corporatism and lack of individualism among the utopians.[24] Later historians have viewed the utopians in the image of the reformers whose innerworldly asceticism Max Weber associated with the beginnings of the Western work ethic.[25] The utopians are perhaps at their most untraditional in their reliance on printed books and in underpinning their democratic institutions with widespread literacy. Recall that in Plato's commonwealth superior knowledge is monopolized by the guardians, and in Augustine's polity the interpretation of scripture is the prerogative of the educated clergy. By contrast, the utopians, like some European reforming religious groups between the Lollards and the Lutherans, earnestly pursue their education and entertainment by means of the written word. They have a working week of some thirty-five hours (six hours a day),[26] and, as this labor is equally divided among all citizens (except slaves), there is plenty of time for the cultivation of the mind. They enjoy themselves rather austerely by going to lectures before daybreak, possibly in imitation of monastic rituals. Through the combination of religious and secular education, More thus incorporates into his design both the Catholic principle of moral instruction by means of an established priesthood and the reformist view that believers should be instructed in the rudiments of literacy in order to educate themselves.

However, if More is unmedieval in his approach to this aspect of religious education, he nonetheless reflects the last centuries of the Middle Ages in his use of contemplative practice. In the view of Augustine, Benedict, and Gregory the Great, a meditative state of mind is achieved chiefly through reading and reflecting on the texts of the Bible. This is what Augustine teaches himself in the *Confessions* as he passes progressively through different schools of philosophy and religion, and it is an extension of this reading program that is outlined in the opening chapters of *The City of God*, book 11. For Augustine, therefore, as for his medieval successors in the tradition of *lectio divina*, there is a coincidence between the highest textual authority and the point of departure for religious contemplation.

By contrast, in More meditation is based on the later tradition of *lectio spiritualis*, which I discuss in the next chapter. This is a type of reading that does not necessarily return to the message of the biblical text, but, basing itself on a variety of biblical and nonbiblical writings, leads the reader on an internal voyage into his or her mental processes. A good example, doubtless inspired by the meditative practices of the Charterhouse, is More's meditation on faith, hope, and charity in the *Dialogue of Comfort*. In this work, we observe the typical result of *lectio spiritualis*, which is not a mental elevation of a Plotinian or Augustinian type, freeing the subject from all worldly constraints, but rather an extended mental exercise that results in an internal narrative in words or images that can be turned outward toward devotional activities. The most original conception in More's *Utopia* may not have been his "communism," for which there are precedents in ancient and medieval thought, but his transformation of this ascetic exercise into a program for achieving social change. It was the beginning of a new era in the utilization of discourse in political philosophy.

As an addendum to this suggestion, let us observe that the literary form of *Utopia* is untraditional in relation to both the ancient and the late ancient approaches to discourse in thinkers like Plato and Augustine. Although the *Republic* is longer than some other Platonic dialogues, it nonetheless adheres to the Socratic principle of solving philosophical problems through a series of questions and answers. The work may have been intended to be read and studied as well as performed, but its literary setting creates above all the impression of oral spontaneity. The participants do not reason from arguments in books, nor do they refer to previous thinkers whose works might have been accessible only in written form. The just society is created by reason and maintained over time by institutions that incorporate rational solutions arrived at through open discussion.

It can be argued that book 1 of *Utopia* resembles a Socratic dialogue, especially in its use of irony.[27] However, books 1 and 2, taken together, more closely parallel the adaptation of the ancient dialogue in Augustine's early writings, such as *De Ordine* or *De Magistro*. In these works a period of open discussion involving the participants is followed by a monologue in which Augustine proposes a solution to the philosophical problem that has been taken up. This type of instruction frequently replaced the Socratic dialogue in the late ancient and medieval periods, especially as Latin became a literary language that was accessible only by means of the written word.[28] The initial discussion among the participants in this didactic genre is comparable to *Utopia*, book 1. The dogmatic statement that accompanies the opening discussion is comparable to Raphael's systematic outline of the institutions of Utopia in book 2.

In both cases the first part of such a dialogue is a conversation,[29] not a logical presentation as in the *Republic*.[30] Also, in contrast to Plato, there is an emphasis on the role of an external audience in judging the truth claims of the participants, whereas in the *Republic* the primary audience consists of those present at the gathering (whatever other audiences may be envisaged). In another late ancient dialogue, *The Consolation of Philosophy*, the comparable role of the external audience is played by Philosophia; with Boethius in mind, the same literary function reappears in Petrarch's *Secretum* as the part played by Truth. *Utopia* is something of a hybrid in this tradition: in book 1, the "Socratic" part, the role of the oral audience is represented by the conversation with Peter Gilles; in book 2, the "dogmatic" part, its role is taken over by the potential readers, who presumably include among their number those who have taken part in the initial conversation. It is this "reader-reformer" who judges the value of the discussion of the Platonic theme of social justice that is common to the two books.[31]

This is a humanist design that takes us far from the situation of Augustine in writing about an ideal or eternal city. In *The City of God* we find ourselves in a vast library of ancient writings, in which Augustine is alone, reading, thinking, and dictating to his secretaries. The scene recalls the situation in which he found himself in *Confessions* 7, in 386, when he compared the Latin translations of Plotinus and John in order to sort out the parallels and differences between pagan and Christian neoplatonism. Augustine had of course heard of the fall of the eternal city of Rome, and, as Christian refugees streamed into Africa, he was genuinely moved by their plight. Yet the real subject of *The City of God* is not this distant calamity, but problems of time, eternity, and history on which he had been reflecting since his conversion to the religious life in 386–387. *The City of God* is the great final work in which he returns to the themes of his youth—the dialogues of Cicero, the intellectual temptations of Greek philosophy, and the elitist paganism of Symmachus, Albinus, and Praetextatus, which was recorded nostalgically in the *Saturnalia* of Macrobius. Augustine was not unmoved by the fall of Rome, but he was not deluded as to its significance. In his view it was an oracle: proof that it was folly for any worldly institution to aspire to true permanence. He told his congregation in Hippo not to be astonished. Cities were like people, who were born, grew to maturity, and got old. Just as the elderly complain of their ailments, Rome was crying out in agony as it prepared to die.[32]

It is not contemporary paganism that Augustine attacks in *The City of God*; it is the beliefs of the pagan past. "It seems," Peter Brown observes, "as if Augustine were demolishing a paganism that existed only in libraries."[33] In his learned response, Augustine develops the theme of the two cities from the biblical account of the creation of man and woman (12.1) and follows it consistently through the Old and New Testaments. This too is a study of past beliefs, a conversation between an author and a library of biblical texts. The relation established between the claims of dialogic reason and textual authority is quite different from what it is in Plato. In the *Republic* Plato expresses his confidence above all in the authority of reason, whereas in *The City of God* Augustine makes a case in favor of the reason of authority. As paganism is opposed by Christianity, ancient verbal logic is answered by Augustine's pessimistic hermeneutics, which proposes that our understanding of texts is like our understanding of time and language—fragmentary and incomplete.

More's view of his potential audience was no less elitist than Augustine's, but it was based on the rather different assumptions of irony and satire. On the one hand, he was heir to the gloomy outlook that was bequeathed to the Middle Ages in the name of Augustine. This attitude is expressed in *De Quatuor Novissimis* in 1522 and *A Dialogue of Comfort Against Tribulation* in 1534, works that are untempered by the progressive view of human abilities proposed in the Aristotelian synthesis of Thomas Aquinas, which was so influential on the ethical thought of the late Middle Ages. On the other hand, there is no counterpart in More of Augustine's conception of his readership along two lines: pagan readers, whom he is trying to dissuade, and Christian readers, frightened by the events in Rome, whose faith he is trying to confirm. Augustine includes much of what one has to know of pagan and Christian history within the twenty-two books of *The City of God*, whereas *Utopia*, book 2, possibly in imitation of Plato, has no quotations, only facts and analysis. In order to appreciate Hythloday's description of the institutions of Utopia, the reader has to be familiar with the institutions of More's England, to which they are frequently opposed. This is what Augustine had in mind when he spoke of an alienated world, and, by means of the foreignness of Utopia, More draws attention to the familiar reality of that alienness. *Utopia* is designed as a stage in the intellectual development of a Christian humanist, just as *The City of God* was a stage in the development of the late ancient Christian apologist. But in More the library is not in the text, as it is in *The City of God*; it is in the reader, and without the presence of this knowledge, *Utopia* loses much of its satirical force.

There remains the question of what More expected the reader to take from *Utopia*. On that issue, there have been numerous opinions over the years. For some historians *Utopia* is a political treatise, while others view the work primarily in a religious or theological context. There is perhaps a way of reconciling these views, and, as a conclusion to this essay I offer a small piece of evidence that points toward this possibility. Earlier I made reference to R. W. Chambers's statement to the effect that *Utopia* presents a society based on the four pagan virtues while not making mention of the three Christian virtues, which, according to traditional thinking, cannot be found in a society based on reason alone. What Chambers clearly knew but omitted to say is that More's discussion of faith, hope, and charity had to await the publication of *A Dialogue of Comfort* some eighteen years later.

The third part of this work is More's longest commentary on the subject. It is tempting to think that he chose deliberately to discuss the four pagan virtues in one place and the three Christian virtues in another, thereby dividing the themes of his writings as he appears to some observers to have divided his life into public and private spheres.[34] If this interpretation is correct, then he would have been what his contemporary Robert Wittinton called him, a man for all seasons. However, if we can extend that metaphor, the weight of the evidence about More's life and writings suggests that he attempted to make the changing seasons of the English court, so to speak, conform to his early Christian ideal of what ethical conduct should be. In this interpretation, *Utopia* and *A Dialogue of Comfort* can be envisaged as parts of the same project, which sees the reform of society as a short-term practical goal while the preservation of spiritual values is something to be sought in the long term. For More, the problem was not only how to create a rational society, but how to prevent the creation of a society that was only rational: a society which, with respect to spiritual values, was literally *utopia*, no place. More did not solve that problem. Nor, for that matter, have we.

Chapter Seven
Lectio Spiritualis

We live at a time when the classical curriculum is disappearing from primary education in all European countries. We cannot expect classical languages to play as large a role as they have in the past in anchoring the national cultures of Europe in a common heritage. It is worth considering the consequences of this development for the understanding of European identity.

The most important classical language to take into consideration is of course Latin. The study of European identity by means of the relationship between Latin and the Romance languages has been an important topic in philology and linguistics for about a hundred and fifty years. The foundations were laid by Friedrich Diez, who published the three volumes of his *Grammatik der romanischen Sprachen* between 1836 and 1843. These studies extended the research of François Raynouard, who produced the *Grammaire de la langue romane* in 1816 and the six-volume *Lexique roman ou dictionnaire de la langue des troubadours comparée avec les autres langues de l'Europe latine* between 1838 and 1844. In 1862 Gaston Paris, a sometime student of Diez in Bonn, published his *Étude sur le rôle de l'accent latin dans la langue française.* Between 1882 and 1885 Graziado Isaia Ascoli published *L'Italia dialettale* in the *Archivio glottologico italiano.*

Herder, the Schlegels, Coleridge, and other romantic thinkers were convinced that the identity of a people is reflected in its language and literature. Their theories were given a linguistic foundation by Wilhelm von Humboldt, who distinguished between language as an objective entity (*ergon*) and as a living force (*energeia*). He also reinstated the view originally expressed by Augustine in *De Trinitate*, book 15, according to which there is a connection between articulated sound and expressed thought by means of an *innere Sprachform*. Humboldt's writings, together with the essays of Benedetto Croce on linguistics and aesthetics, influenced the views of Karl Vossler and his eminent students, Leo Spitzer and Victor Klemperer, the latter of whom won posthumous fame for his memoir on the deformation of the language of daily life in Nazi Germany. The intellectual crisis of World War II gave rise to a number of important studies on relations between the Romance languages and cultural history, among them the celebrated volumes of Ernst Robert Curtius and Erich Auerbach. Speaking of the significance of Croce, Vossler, Curtius, Spitzer, and possibly himself, Auerbach remarked in 1957 that "their breadth of vision justifies us in calling these men *European* philologists."[1]

The vision to which Auerbach referred included literature written in Latin as well as in the vernacular languages. This approach is well exemplified in Curtius's *Europäische Literatur und lateinisches Mittelalter*, which was published in 1948 and dedicated to the memory of Gustav Gröber and Aby Warburg, who died respectively in 1911 and 1929. It is possible to argue that the venerable collaboration between the history of Latin and the Romance languages had entered a period of troubled relations at the time at which Auerbach, Curtius, and Spitzer were presenting the case in favor of a "European" philology. The generations that followed the war produced not an outright divorce but a polite separation in which students of Latin and the Romance languages became increasingly specialized. As a consequence they took less and less interest in each other's disciplines. At the risk of playing the part of a marriage counselor who is somewhat out of touch with the mores of his times, I would like to take the occasion of this concluding chapter to suggest that it may not be too late to save the union. It is imperative to do so if there is to be any lasting understanding of the historical origins of the European identity, to say nothing of its perpetuation by means of education. As a modest contribution to this reuniting of interests, I would like to discuss a subject whose history is equally divided between the Latin Middle Ages and the Romance literatures from Dante to Petrarch: this is the use of reading and writing as forms of contemplative practice.

*   *   *

Let me begin with an example of what I mean by the use of reading and writing as contemplative practice.

In the opening chapter of the *Soliloquies*, written in all probability in 387,[2] we find Augustine engaged in reflection with himself on his own behalf (*volventi mihi . . . ac . . . mecum*): he is inquiring earnestly into himself (*memetipsum*) and into what might be good for him, as contrasted with the evils that he hopes to avoid.

He hears a voice: he does not know whether it is he who is speaking or someone else, or whether the voice comes from outside or inside his mind (*extrinsecus sive intrinsecus*). While he attempts to find the answer to these questions, the voice is identified as the allegorical representation of his reason. She asks him what he would do if he discovered something during his reflections and wished to preserve it before he proceeded to other matters. Augustine replies that he would record the insight in his memory, but Reason points out that his memory may not be large enough to contain everything that is produced by his thinking (*omnia excogitata*).

She recommends instead that the insight in question be written down (*scribendum est*). But she adds that Augustine is at present too weak for the labor of writing (*scribendi labor*). Moreover, in her view, the type of reflection in which he has been engaged is not suitable for dictation but requires his complete solitude.[3] What is he to do? Reason's advice is to pray, and to commit his prayer to writing (*Ora . . . et hoc ipsum litteris manda*). The written text, when reread, will act as a form of encouragement. Augustine is also advised to sum up what he has discovered in a few brief conclusions.[4] Finally, in passing from the first to the second step, he should not be concerned with reaching a large common readership (*turba legentium*), but with recording a few sayings for his own companions (*cives*).

This chapter is an interesting departure from Hellenistic contemplative practices as they are found in authors Augustine would have known, such as Cicero, Seneca, and Plotinus.[5] Augustine initially adheres to an ancient literary convention in portraying himself in a state of meditation on himself and his ethical situation. However, there is no precedent for the type of literary genre that follows, which he calls by a new word, a *soliloquium*.[6] In this internal dialogue, Reason distinguishes between oral and written forms of record, favoring the latter, and divides the writing of what Augustine has discovered in his reflections into two stages: an extended version, represented by the neoplatonic prayer that follows in chapter 2, and a conclusion, which is found in chapter 1 of book 2. There Augustine summarizes his lengthy prayer in the statement, "Deus semper idem, noverim me, noverim te. Oratum est" (Ever changeless God, may I know myself, may I know you: that is my prayer). As a reward for following her instructions, Reason leads him in a Socratic manner through the proof for the *cogito.*

The writing of this essay would have been greatly simplified if there were a continuous tradition of the use of such contemplative practices leading from Augustine to Petrarch, who puts comparable recommendations in the mouth of Augustinus in dialogue 2 of the *Secretum.* This type of reflection is not absent during the Middle Ages: it is found in Boethius and in the meditative prayers of Anselm of Canterbury and William of St. Thierry, which are largely Augustinian in inspiration. However, the development of contemplative practices during the centuries that followed Augustine normally takes place within the devotional exercises associated with the reading of scripture. The type of reading that is involved with mental exercises is not *lectio divina* itself, which provides the framework for these devotions, but a subdivision that has been called *lectio spiritualis,* in which a great deal of attention is paid to methods of meditating on words and images.[7] On the whole, it is *lectio spiritualis* that provides the theological background for the reading and writing practices that appear in vernacular literature after the publication of Dante's *De Vulgari Eloquentia* in 1305.

As a consequence, it is possible to argue that it was not only the presence of the Latin language that shaped European cultural identity in the centuries after Augustine, but a particular way of reading that language in spiritual writings during the period in which the Romance languages became an important vehicle for expressing a concern with identity through literature. Wherever the meditative or contemplative mode of thought associated with *lectio spiritualis* was prevalent, an identity could be shaped by peoples who did not have the same linguistic roots, for example the medieval speakers of the different Romance and Germanic languages, because the practitioners of these exercises had been taught to meditate on words and images in essentially the same way.

There is no simple way to define what medieval authors understood by *lectio spiritualis,* since few authors used the term in a technical manner before the fourteenth century. The best way to approach the subject is through the concept of *lectio divina*, which has well-known roots in the patristic period.

According to Jean Leclercq, the author of a classic study of the subject,[8] the founders of the medieval tradition of *lectio divina* were Benedict and Gregory the Great. However, the methods that they employed had precedents in the biblical period in both Hebrew and Greek. A text that combines these traditions is Romans 10:8, where Paul, in contrasting Jewish law and Christian faith, supports his position with a quotation from Deuteronomy 30:14 that refers to the presence of God's word in the believer's "mouth or heart." It was the recreation of the biblical text through oral reading and recitation that provided the rationale for *lectio divina* as it evolved out of Jewish tradition into Christianity. In a statement that was echoed by (among others) Evagrius Ponticus and John Cassian, Cyprian emphasized the oral nature of the experience and its closeness to prayer: "Sit tibi vel oratio assidua vel lectio: nunc cum Deo loquere, nunc Deus tecum" (May you engage constantly in prayer or reading: in the one you speak with God, in the other God speaks with you).[9] It was Origen and Augustine who were chiefly responsible for expanding the biblical and early patristic notions of *lectio divina* into a more systematic style of asceticism. This tradition was passed on to the Middle Ages as a part of the divine office. From the eleventh century, it became customary for monastic authors to speak of three interconnected ascetic activities, *lectio*, *meditatio*, and *oratio*.[10]

It is important to stress that during the Middle Ages *lectio divina* was not a type of interpretation, that is, a branch of exegesis, hermeneutics, or theology. It was a contemplative practice that brought together the Hellenistic tradition of spiritual exercises and the meditative reading that characterized Jewish and Christian devotional traditions. As time passed, it was inevitable that Christian thinkers engaged in *lectio divina* would begin to ask questions about the nature of the interior reflection that was involved: how words and images functioned in the mind during devotions, and how such internal representations could influence lived experience or be influenced by it. This type of thinking gave rise to what was later called *lectio spiritualis*. As it evolved over time, *lectio spiritualis* did not develop into a separate tradition, but it came to differ from *lectio divina* in a number of ways that have to do with internal words and images in a contemplative context. At the risk of presenting a somewhat schematic picture of this development, I should like to try to summarize these differences.

First of all, in *lectio divina* continuity arose, as noted, between reading, meditation, and prayer, whereas in *lectio spiritualis* it occurred on the frontier between reading, interior reflection, and a number of other devotional activities. In *lectio divina* the reflective process began in the presence of the text, whereas in *lectio spiritualis* it could take place in the absence of the text; that is, it could be based entirely on internal resources. The presence of the biblical text was therefore a necessary condition for *lectio divina* but only a sufficient condition for *lectio spiritualis*. In the one meditation focused on the words that were actually read; in the other it was concerned with words or images that arose during or after the reading. Also, in *lectio divina* the passage of time was marked by the sounds of the words that were read, as in Augustine's famous measurement of time in book 11 of the *Confessions*; in *lectio spiritualis* it was measured by what Edmund Husserl called internal time-consciousness, whose ebb and flow was entirely determined by the subject. If *lectio divina* created an experience in which silence succeeded sound, *lectio spiritualis* frequently took place entirely in silence.

In *lectio divina* reading was not an autonomous activity; it was one form of asceticism among others. According to Jerome, Origen and his brethren meditated in the morning; they read the Bible together during meals and before going to bed.[11] In Anthony *theia anagnosis* was synonymous with *meletao*, that is, to train or study, in the sense of exercising the mind or practicing a spiritual exercise; and with *philologeo*, meaning to study, to pursue wisdom, or to think about scripture.[12] Benedict, too, speaks in a single phrase of *meditare aut legere*.[13] By contrast, in *lectio spiritualis*, *lectio* and *studium* played somewhat different roles: the one was concerned with the text, the other with the reader's response. *Lectio spiritualis* was thus an inner discipline that could involve self-exploration on the part of the subject as an aspect of his or her spiritual progress.

This exploration could produce a spiritual autobiography, as a transcript of the subject's emotions and experiences and as an object of meditation itself; examples include William of St. Thierry's *Epistola ad Fratres de Monte Dei de Vita Solitaria* and Bonaventure's *Itinerarium Mentis in Deum*. In the Franciscan David of Augsburg or the Dominican Humbert of Romans, spiritual progress was brought about by ascetical activities that were the result of contemplation but not necessarily the direct result of the reading of biblical texts. In these authors, one might argue that the reading process acquired an autonomous status, since a separation was acknowledged between reading and the other devotional activities that were associated with it. Reading also meant texts other than the Bible, and these presumably were not all read in the same way, as was the case in *lectio divina*. A late definition of *lectio spiritualis* does not specifically mention the books of the Bible as objects of spiritual reading: "We call spiritual reading (*lectio spiritualis*) the activity in which we open and read mystical books or spiritual treatises. In this activity we seek not only information concerning spiritual matters but preferably in addition their flavor and emotional content."[14]

Finally, let me observe in the light of this definition that, if *lectio divina* focused on content and constantly returned the reader to the biblical original, *lectio spiritualis* was chiefly concerned with expression, as an outgrowth of the individual's affective life. This meant that there was a different attitude toward the emotions. *Lectio divina* was a way of controlling, managing, or reshaping the emotions; this function was described by John Cassian, who spoke frequently of the ways in which the desert fathers mastered negative emotions like sadness or boredom.[15] By contrast, *lectio spiritualis* was a way of experiencing emotions and of creating an awareness of emotional experience as it was taking place. As a consequence of this difference, in *lectio divina* emotions were judged to be positive or negative in relation to the subject's spiritual state before reading took place, whereas in *lectio spiritualis* they acquired their ethical status progressively in the context of reading and contemplation. In *lectio spiritualis* but not in *lectio divina*, therefore, one can speak of a subjectively organized narrative of the emotions that is enacted in the reader's mind. In *lectio divina* the subject's thoughts and emotions were diminished in importance, while the emotions expressed in the biblical text were emphasized; in *lectio spiritualis* the subject's awareness of his or her thoughts and emotions increased in the light of the consideration that was given to the biblical text. As a consequence, two pathways toward meaning emerged in *lectio spiritualis*, one deriving from the text, the other from the reader. In the latter spiritual progress arose as a result of the manner in which the individual reacted emotionally to the presence of spiritual thinking itself.

In sum, in *lectio divina* the centralizing element in the contemplative process was the biblical text itself. This was the constant reference point for the author's reflections and therefore for his or her conception of literary identity. In *lectio spiritualis* the centralizing element was the thinking subject, who was the source of the continuity of the contemplative process and therefore the source of literary identity. One sign of this emphasis appears in authors who mentioned among their recommendations the reading of edifying works other than the Bible. In Jean Gerson's *De Libris Legendis a Monacho,* for instance, these included the *Vitae Patrum,* Bernard of Clairvaux, the *Moralia* of Gregory the Great, Richard and Hugh of St. Victor, and above all Bonaventure.[16] A separate list of morally instructive writings was provided by Gerson for a secular prince.[17] Spokesmen on behalf of *lectio spiritualis* likewise offered synthetic summaries of earlier meditative techniques, especially those employed in *lectio divina;* these were published as handbooks for both religious and laypersons. A remarkable example is the *Rosetum Exercitorum Spiritualium* of Jean Mombaer, who died in 1501; its publication preceded by only thirty-three years the founding of the Society of Jesus based on the *Spiritual Exercises* of Ignatius of Loyola. This period of consolidation in the history of *lectio spiritualis* runs roughly from the founding of the Devotio Moderna in the fourteenth century to the high spirituality of François de Sales, who died in 1622.

*   *   *

I should stress again that this is a rather schematic summary of the features of *lectio spiritualis.* No two authors engaged in this type of exercise interpreted it in precisely the same way. However, even within the limitations of such a presentation it is easy to see how the inner concern with words and images in *lectio spiritualis* could be connected with comparable developments in the Romance literatures. This view is confirmed if a second feature of *lectio spiritualis* is taken into consideration. This is the encouragement of writing as a contemplative practice.

Once again, I should like to approach this problem through the better understood phenomenon of reading. We are familiar nowadays with a number of changes that took place in reading practices during the later Middle Ages. There was a rise in the practice of silent reading, which has been illuminated by the research of Paul Saenger,[18] and a change in the functions of memory, which became less dependent on the voice than on the eye. Still another development was the gradual deinstitutionalization of the reading process. From the time of Benedict to the death of Bernard of Clairvaux in 1153, most books in the field of spirituality were designed to be read in an institutional context. By and large, they were produced in limited manuscript copies and circulated within monastic houses. Only infrequently did codices leave the institutional milieu altogether. Individual book owners were rare, and the books they owned bore the imprint of the institutional setting in which they had arisen. The great biblical commentaries of the period, works of theology and pastoral literature, and even secular writings on literary, scientific, or other nonreligious topics can usually be classified by paleographers according to the religious establishments for which they were designed.

All this began to change from about the middle of the twelfth century. One important force was vernacular preaching, which consisted in the oral reading of scripture in a vernacular language with a simple commentary, making it possible for the Bible to be understood by nonliterates (that is, nonreaders of Latin). Another type of change took place in cathedral schools and the University of Paris, where the reading of books in the curriculum was gradually detached from the institutional affiliations of the students. One read a book not because one belonged to a particular community, but because one was studying a particular subject. Third, the production and consumption of books began to obey the laws of the market. Laypersons and ecclesiastics acquired and maintained personal libraries in which books were not symbolic objects but sources of information on matters pertinent to everyday life such as medicine, estate management, and warfare. Finally, for first time since antiquity, secular authors became aware of the existence of secular audiences.

These changes helped prepare the way for an important transformation in the function of literary composition: the use of writing as a mode of meditation, which became a major type of contemplative exercise in authors between Petrarch and Montaigne. During the early Middle Ages, work in the monastic scriptorium was considered an appropriate type of manual labor. However, from the eleventh century, there was also a revival of Hellenistic attitudes toward the relationship between writing and reflection, which had been a prominent feature of the works of Cicero, Seneca, and Augustine. Othloh of St. Emmeram and Guibert of Nogent spoke of composition as a type of internal narrative or vision that lay somewhere on the boundary between meditation and fantasy. Bernard Silvester and Alan of Lille developed late ancient methods of allegorical personification in which grammar, rhetoric, and metaphors of writing played large roles. By the time of Dante's death in 1321, compositional activities had become a normal routine in the contemplative practices of both religious and secular authors.

One of the influential developments of this technique in the late fourteenth century occurred in the Devotio Moderna. The founder of the movement, Gerard Groote, organized the Brethren of the Common Life to live together as a confraternity near the monastery of the regular Augustinian canons at Windersheim. The brethren started a school at Deventer, whose most celebrated student was Erasmus (between 1475 and 1484). The theology of the Devotio Moderna was essentially traditional; what was new was the intensity of emotional commitment associated with the activity of writing. In addition to running a school, tending the sick, and other works of charity, the brethren were especially devoted to instruction in the art of writing in Latin. The schoolroom became their cell, and writing was their form of silent meditation. The result, in Groote's terms, was a *mentis exercitatio* that brought into play different types of reflection on words and images in an effort to recreate an internal biblical narrative. Thomas à Kempis, one of the celebrated products of the movement, made this technique widely known in *The Imitation of Christ*.

An interesting feature of the late medieval interest in writing as a contemplative practice was the extensive use of images in relation to texts. The association of texts and images is traditionally attributed to Gregory the Great, who likened images to texts for those who could not read in a pair of celebrated letters in 599 and 600. Gregory's statements were frequently quoted during the Middle Ages as a justification for the use of images in worship, in contrast to Byzantine attitudes, which alternated between support of and opposition to iconography. Gregory was highly influenced by Benedict, whose life he wrote, as well as by Augustine, whose ideas inform much of his spirituality. It is reasonable to assume, therefore, that he was speaking of the use of images within *lectio divina*, that is, in the devotional activities of reading, meditation, and prayer, rather than in an independent relationship between texts and images. This option required the development of a different conception of sacred reading in which a series of narrative images in the mind was a potential parallel for an internal narrative text. This was a later medieval and postmedieval development, which had a widespread influence after 1500. It is a short step from the use of this technique in Renaissance devotions to the internally organized religious art of figures like Gian Lorenzo Bernini.

*   *   *

The parallel between words and images as mental representations and as resources for contemplation was instrumental in establishing the connection between the linguistic and theological notions of identity to which I referred at the beginning of this chapter.

For religious authors engaged in *lectio divina* or *lectio spiritualis* the problem of identity arose as an interpretation of Genesis 1:26, in which humans were described as being made in God's "image and likeness." Although there were numerous interpretations of this statement,[19] patristic and medieval theologians were agreed that humans received their identity, that is, their individuality, personality, or distinctiveness, from the moment that they received the *imago Dei* (much in the same way that we nowadays believe that people receive their potential makeup through genetics). According to most thinkers on this theme, men and women had the *imago* obscured but not lost in the Fall, whereas the *similitudo* was destroyed by original sin and is restored in baptism. There was no final agreement on just what was meant by the notion of *imago Dei*. For Gregory of Nyssa it was free will. Augustine thought it resided in the combined powers of the soul, that is, in memory, intellect, and will (representing respectively the Father, the Son, and the Holy Ghost).

In the mystical theology of both the Eastern and the Western churches, the realization of the *imago Dei* was interpreted as the point at which the soul is capable of entering into spiritual union with God. In this respect, there was a harmony of thinking between the theory of image and likeness and the practice of contemplative spirituality by which this union was presumably achieved. A precedent for this type of approach to spiritual union is found in Plotinus, without, however, the connection to the reading process that is typical of Hellenistic Judaism and early Christianity. Plotinus's statements on the union with the One were the subject of

an extensive commentary by Augustine in *Confessions*, book 7, and
De Trinitate, books 8–14. It was in these works, as well as in Augustine's sermons and biblical commentaries, that the reflective reader
emerged as the chief exponent of the theme of spiritual union.
The theoretical approach to the issues advocated by Augustine was
commented upon by the ninth-century thinker Johannes Scottus
Eriugena, who knew the Greek spirituality of Maximus the Confessor and the Pseudo-Denis, and among others by the Victorines
in the twelfth century; however, it was within the system of sacred
reading, that is, in *lectio divina* and *lectio spiritualis,* that its practical
consequences were most widely explored. The problem of identity
subsequently became a topic of meditation and contemplation in a
long list of mystical thinkers, including Bernard of Clairvaux, Bonaventure, and Meister Eckhart. This tradition was extended into the
early modern period by John of the Cross and Teresa of Avila.

During this final period a new element entered the discussion
that was to prove decisive for the future development of identity
as a literary theme. This was the reintroduction of ancient methods
of contemplative practice in the writings of early modern thinkers,
beginning with Petrarch's *Secretum.* Petrarch was thoroughly familiar with the literature on image and likeness in Augustine. Through
the figure of Augustinus in the *Secretum,* he advocated the use of a
type of meditation that is well within the boundaries of *lectio spiritualis.* However, Petrarch was also well acquainted with the ancient
spiritual exercises that preceded the Christian period. As noted, his
defense of Christian contemplative practices is very largely made
through quotations from his two favorite classical sources on the
question, Cicero and Seneca, whose statements on the topic he frequently put into the mouth of Augustinus in defense of Christian
values. We can think of the *Secretum* as a hybrid on the question of
identity: it is a dialogue that is midway between the ancient conception, which is based on self-reliance, and the Augustinian, which
makes the person's "image and likeness" a unique gift from God.

At the center of this problem is a contrast between two types of
reading as well as Petrarch's belief, expressed through Franciscus,
that writing is a valid form of contemplative practice. The issues are
brought to a head toward the end of *Secretum,* book 2.[20] This is the
moment in the dialogue at which Augustinus tells Franciscus that
the confusion he associates with life in the towns is really a confusion within himself. The only way that he can attain tranquillity is

through the practice of meditative exercises. Augustinus suggests a close reading of Seneca's *De Tranquillitate Animae,* Cicero's *Tusculanae,* and Petrarch's own *De Vita Solitaria.* When Franciscus replies that he has read these books, Augustinus asks him whether they have been any help. Yes, while I was reading them, Franciscus says, but once they were out of my hands the positive effects vanished.[21] Augustinus observes that his experience is the typical consequence of the reading practices of his day (*communis legentium mos est*), at least among disreputable literary types (*literatorum . . . flagitiosissimos . . . greges*), who argue a lot over the art of living in the classroom but convert little of this talk into action (*de arte vivendi, multa licet in scolis disputentur, in actum pauca converti*). In his eyes, the problem is not what Franciscus reads, but the way he reads.

For Franciscus texts are evidently not only a means to an end, which is the silence, solitude, and tranquility represented by the meditating figure of Augustinus in the dialogue's preface. They have also become an end in themselves, that is, objects of meditation in a written form, as Reason suggested at the beginning of Augustine's *Soliloquies.* Petrarch's interest in *lectio divina* and *lectio spiritualis* is in part an expression of nostalgia for the monastic life of his brother Gerardo, or perhaps of other friends like Dionigi da Borgo San Sepolchro, who presented him with his copy of Augustine's *Confessions.* Through the figure of Augustinus, he also expresses a yearning for the spiritual exercises of Hellenistic philosophy, which he associates with a comparable ethical position. However, in the end he does not clearly choose either of these traditional answers. To some, this solution is disappointing, since it suggests that the major problem taken up in the *Secretum* is left unresolved. But Petrarch may have designed the work in the Platonic tradition as an aporetic dialogue in which the dual character of Augustinus/Franciscus plays the role of Socrates, telling us not what we know but what we do not know about Petrarch's attempt to achieve otherworldly, contemplative values through the worldly vehicle of secular writing. Like that of Socrates, Petrarch's major legacy may be, not to have answered this question, but to have asked it.

*   *   *

I began this chapter with the mention of E. R. Curtius, a prominent member of a generation of philologists who shaped our understanding of the relationship between the Latin Middle Ages and the Romance languages on the problem of European identity. I would like to conclude with one further reflection on this theme.

In July 1949, just one year after the appearance of *Europäische Literatur und lateinisches Mittelalter*, Curtius delivered a charming lecture on "The Medieval Bases of Western Thought" in Aspen, Colorado, in which he touched briefly on what he considered to be an insurmountable barrier between theology and poetry during the Middle Ages. His example was Thomas Aquinas, who wrote a series of splendid hymns for the feast of Corpus Christi but who, in Curtius's view, considered them to be "sacred song" rather than "poetry." If a philosopher of the quality of Thomas was able to look on his own poetry in this light, what would his successors have thought of the poetry of Dante? Curtius's conclusion was that the attitude of serious thinkers in the Middle Ages toward such "scribblers" of verse would have been one of "supreme indifference."

The material I have presented here, albeit somewhat summarily, suggests a more nuanced interpretation of relations between theology and literature during the Middle Ages based on the criteria furnished by the history of contemplative practice. For Curtius's generation, philosophy or theology in this period was largely identified with systematic thinking. However, much of the writing I have discussed, while eminently theological, is rather unsystematic in nature: it is episodic and occasional, often consisting of what we would nowadays call essays (or assays) in the tradition of Augustine, Erasmus, Montaigne, and Pascal. This was one of the major ways thoughtful individuals introduced contemplative practice into their reflections on the problem of the European identity between the fourth and the seventeenth century. It is a major, unrecognized tradition in ethics that developed out of the late medieval habit of *lectio spiritualis*. In my view, this tradition is worth recovering before it fades entirely from view with the teaching of classical languages out of which it arose.

Notes

Chapter 1. Reading and Self-Knowledge

1. This chapter is a translation and revision of my inaugural lecture at the Collège de France (see the Acknowledgments section). I would like to acknowledge a debt to the writings of three former professors in that institution, Étienne Gilson, Pierre Courcelle, and Michel Foucault. I am likewise grateful for helpful conversations with Yves Bonnefoy, Harald Weinrich, Michel Zink, and above all Pierre Hadot.

2. The English translation of this lecture by Michael Chase appeared as "Forms of Life and Forms of Discourse in Ancient Philosophy," in *Philosophy as a Way of Life: Spiritual Exercises from Socrates to Foucault*, ed. and intro. Arnold I. Davidson (Oxford, 1995), 49–77, at 59 (my translation).

3. *Moralia in Iob*, 1.33.

4. *L'amour des lettres et le désir de Dieu* (Paris, 1957), 23.

5. *Space Between Words: The Origins of Silent Reading* (Stanford, Calif.,1997).

6. *Confessiones* 6.3.3.

7. *Auteurs spirituels et textes dévots du Moyen Age latin* (Paris, 1932), 191n5.

8. *De Doctrina Christiana, prooemium*, 4.

9. *A Book of Showings*, c. 2, ed. Edmund Colledge and James Walsh, Pt. 2 (Toronto, 1978), 285.

10. *Sur la lecture* (Paris, 1989), 29–30.

Chapter 2. Ethical Values and the Literary Imagination

1. Examples of this renewed interest include Julia Annas, *The Morality of Happiness* (New York, 1993) and *Platonic Ethics, Old and New* (Ithaca, N.Y., 1999); Brad Inwood, *Ethics and Human Action in Early Stoicism* (Oxford, 1985); Martha Nussbaum, *The Fragility of Goodness: Luck and Ethics in Greek Tragedy and Philosophy* (Cambridge, 1986) and *The Therapy of Desire: Theory and Practice in Hellenistic Ethics* (Princeton, N.J., 1994); and Bernard Williams, *Shame and Necessity*, Sather Classical Lectures 57 (Berkeley, Calif.,

1993). On late ancient thought two studies of interest are John M. Rist, *Augustine: Ancient Thought Baptized* (Cambridge, 1994); and John Magee, *Boethius on Signification and Mind*, Philosophia Antiqua 52 (Leiden, 1989). On the background of the issues discussed in this chapter, see A. A. Long, "The Socratic Legacy" and Brad Inwood and Pierluigi Donini, "Stoic Ethics" in *The Cambridge History of Hellenistic Philosophy*, ed. Keimpe Algra, Jonathan Barnes, Japp Mansfield, and Malcolm Scholfield (Cambridge, 1999), respectively pp. 617–41, 675–738.

2. *European Literature and the Latin Middle Ages*, trans. Willard R. Trask (New York, 1963), Excursus 5: "Late Antique Literary Studies," 436–45.

3. On this topic, see above all Pierre Hadot, *Qu'est-ce que la philosophie antique?* (Paris, 1995), and, for an outstanding study of a Hellenistic thinker, Pierre Hadot, *La citadelle intérieure: Introduction aux Pensées de Marc Aurèle* (Paris, 1992), especially chapter 3, "Les Pensées comme exercises spirituels."

4. On the continuities, see Hadot, *Qu'est-ce la philosophie antique?*, 265–378.

5. These are emphasized by Michel Foucault, *Histoire de la sexualité*, vol. 3, *Le souci de soi* (Paris, 1984). For a review of Foucault's ideas on later ancient thought and their relationship to the better informed views of Pierre Hadot, see Arnold I. Davidson, "Ethics as Ascetics: Foucault, the History of Ethics, and Ancient Thought," in *Foucault and the Writing of History*, ed. Jan Goldstein (Cambridge, Mass., 1990), 63–80. For an important criticism of Foucault's reading of ancient texts, see Hadot's essay in that volume, "Reflections on the Idea of the 'Cultivation of the Self,'" 206–13.

6. Jerome Bruner, *Acts of Meaning*, Jerusalem-Harvard Lectures (Cambridge, Mass., 1990), 31.

7. This is the view on ethics, intentions, and the self that Charles Taylor expresses forcefully in *Sources of the Self: The Making of the Modern Identity* (Cambridge, Mass., 1989).

8. *Vita Plotini*, 1.5–10, discussed in the next chapter.

9. Cf. Xenophon, *Memorabilia* 4.4.5, where comparable views on the problem of teaching justice are attributed to Socrates.

10. As suggested in *Letter* 7.2.4–5, in which Augustine contrasts *phantasiae* and *phantasmata*; ed. Alois Goldbacher, *Corpus Scriptorum Ecclesiasticorum Latinorum* 33.2, 15–16. On the relationship of such images to language in Stoic thought, see Gerard Watson, *Phantasia in Classical Thought* (Galway, 1988), 49–50, 53, 56.

11. Gilbert Ryle, *Plato's Progress* (Cambridge, 1966), 44.

12. See Siegfried Sudhaus, "Epikur als Beichtvater," *Archiv für Religionswissenschaft* 14 (1911): 647–48; W. Schmid, "Contritio und 'Ultima linea rerum' in neuen epikureischen Texten," *Rheinisches Museum* 100 (1957): 301–27.

13. Graham Greene, *The End of the Affair* (London, 1951), beginning chapter 1.

14. For a discussion, see my study, *Augustine the Reader: Meditation, Self-Knowledge, and the Ethics of Interpretation* (Cambridge, Mass., 1996), 43–74.

Chapter 3. Later Ancient Literary Realism

1. Reference to these works is understood to be made to *Mimesis: Dargestellte Wirklichkeit in der abendländischen Literatur* (Bern, 1959 [1946]) and *Literatursprache und Publikum in der lateinischen Spätantike und im Mittelalter* (Bern, 1959), For convenience I quote the standard English translations respectively of Willard Trask (Princeton, N.J., 1953) and Ralph Manheim (New York, 1965). The bibliography of Auerbach's writings is conveniently summarized in his *Gesammelte Aufsätze zur romanischen Philologie* (Bern, 1967), 365–69.

2. (Leipzig, 1915; 2nd ed. 1923). This is his most frequently cited secondary work.

3. "Figura," *Archivum Romanicum* 22 (1939): 436–89; "Sacrae scripturae sermo humilis," *Neuphilologische Mitteilungen* 42 (1941): 57–67 and *Garp Filolojileri Dergisi* 1 (1947):15–22; "Sermo humilis I," *Romanische Forschungen* 64 (1952), 304–64; "Lateinische Prosa des 9. und 10. Jahrhunderts (Sermo humilis II)," *Romanische Forschungen* 66 (1954): 1–64.

4. See the fundamental studies of Pierre Hadot, *Marius Victorinus: Recherches sur sa vie et ses oeuvres* (Paris, 1971), 201–10 and *Porphyre et Victorinus*, 2 vols. (Paris, 1968).

5. For a succinct review of the considerable literature on this subject, see Goulven Madec, *Saint Augustin et la philosophie: Notes critiques* (Paris, 1992), 27–33.

6. Cf. Pierre Hadot, *Plotin ou la simplicité du regard* (Paris, 1973), 21–39, esp. 26.

7. *Vita Plotini*, 1.1. I utilize the edition and translation of A. H. Armstrong in the Loeb Classical Library, *Plotinus*, vol. 1, 2nd ed. (Cambridge, Mass., 1989), which incorporates the changes in Henry-Schwyzer, *Plotini Opera*, vol. 3 (Oxford, 1982).

8. On his views, see A. H. Armstrong, "Plotinus, Amelius, and Porphyry," in *The Cambridge History of Later Greek and Early Medieval Philosophy*, ed. Armstrong (Cambridge, 1967), 264–68.

9. *Vita*, 1.5–10, trans. Armstrong, Loeb, vol. 1, p. 3. Plotinus's followers may have had in mind the veneration of images of Epicurus in paintings and on rings. The practice was noted by Cicero, *De Finibus*, 5.1.3, and by Seneca, *Epistulae Morales*, 25.5. On the spread of such images and their rationale, see Bernard Frischer, *The Sculpted Word: Epicureanism and Philosophical Recruitment in Ancient Greece* (Berkeley, Calif., 1982), 87–128. Also, because Porphyry has in part selected events from the life of Plotinus for their rhetorical effect, one should not rule out the possibility that the anecdote is intended to give an authoritative voice to his personal dislike of Christian practices, among them the worship of images of Christ.

10. Ibid., 4.10.

11. Ibid., 3.35.

12. Cf. Pierre Hadot, *La citadelle intérieure: Introduction aux Pensées de Marc Aurèle* (Paris, 1992), 8–9, and, on the notion of oral "spiritual exercises," see his essay, "La philosophie antique: Une éthique ou une pratique?" in *Problèmes de la morale antique*, ed. Paul Demont (Amiens, 1993), 7–37.

13. An observation that may in part be rhetorical, as it draws attention to the need for someone—namely Porphyry—to bring order to the discussion.

14. *Vita*, 7.1, p. 24.

15. Ibid., 8.1–8, p. 28.

16. Ibid., 13.1–6, p. 38.

17. I make the claim with caution; for a description of the parameters of dyslexia, see Insup Taylor and M. Martin Taylor, *The Psychology of Reading* (New York, 1983), 421–28, which is however limited to empirical research on dyslexic children.

18. *Mimesis* (New York, 1953), 59–60. The questions arising from Auerbach's handling of another violent scene, the description of the arrest of Peter Valvomeres in Ammianus Marcellinus, *Res Gestae* XV, are cogently reviewed by Timothy D. Barnes, *Ammianus Marcellinus and the Representation of Historical Reality* (Ithaca, N.Y. and London, 1998), 11–19.

19. For a summary of the evidence, see Pierre Courcelle, *Recherches sur les Confessions de saint Augustin*, 2nd ed. (Paris, 1968), 30–32. For a refutation of Courcelle's view, see James J. O'Donnell, *Augustine: Confessions* (Oxford, 1992), vol. 2, 360–62.

20. Diogenes Laertius, *Vitae Philosophorum* 4.16, ed. H. S. Long (Oxford, 1964), vol. 1, 173. Augustine's source could have been Horace, *Sat.*, 2.3.253–57. On the place of the story among ancient conversions to philosophy, see Olof Gigon, "Antike Erzählungen über die Berufung zur Philosophie," *Museum Helveticum* 3 (1946): 19–20; on its symbolic significance, see Jean-Paul Dumont, "Les modèles de conversion à la philosophie chez Diogène Laërce," *Augustinus* 32 (1987): 88.

21. Augustine's conclusion invites comparison with Seneca, *Ep. ad Lucilium* 7.8, in which the brutality of interim entertainments at the games leads the philosopher to advise his friend: "Recede in te ipsum, quantum potes."

22. See the dossier complied by Pierre Courcelle, "Tradition néo-platonicienne et traditions chrétiennes de la 'région de dissemblance' (Platon, *Politique* 273 d)," *Archives d'histoire doctrinale et littéraire du moyen âge*, année 1957 (1958): 5–33.

23. *Vita* 3.13–24.

24. Ibid., 7.32–39.

25. Ibid., 9.6–9.

26. Ibid., 9.16–23.

27. Ibid., 12.1–3.

28. Ibid., 12.3–10.

29. *Confessiones* 5.8.

30. Ibid., 2.1–20.

31. *Dante als Dichter der irdischen Welt* (Berlin, 1929); trans. Ralph Manheim, *Dante: Poet of the Secular World* (Chicago, 1961).

32. See Mary Carruthers, *The Book of Memory: A Study in Medieval Culture* (Cambridge, 1990), and Janet Coleman, *Ancient and Medieval Memories: Studies in the Reconstruction of the Past* (Cambridge, 1992). A classic in the

field remains Francis A. Yates, *The Art of Memory* (London, 1966). On Augustine's notion of memory and his transformation (and criticism) of neoplatonic views, see A. Solignac, "La mémoire selon saint Augustin," in *Les Confessions VIII–XIII*, Bibliothèque Augustinienne, 2nd ser. 14 (Paris, 1962), 557–67.

Chapter 4. The Problem of Self-Representation

1. References in this section are to *Epistulae Morales ad Lucilium*, ed. L. D. Reynolds, 2 vols. (Oxford, 1966), and Marcus Aurelius, *Meditations*, ed. A. S. L. Farquarson, 2 vols. (Oxford, 1944).

2. *Ep.*, 46.1: "Tanta autem dulcedine me tenuit et traxit ut illum sine ulla dilatione perlegerim."

3. *Marc Aurèle: Écrits pour lui-même*, ed. Pierre Hadot and Concetta Luna (Paris, 1998), Introduction générale, xxxviii–xxxix.

4. Pierre Hadot, *La citadelle intérieure: Introduction aux Pensées de Marc Aurèle* (Paris, 1992), 38–39.

5. *Ep.*, 40.1 and Héloïse, *Ep.*, 1, in *Historia Calamitatum: Texte critique avec une introduction*, ed. Jacques Monfrin, 2nd ed. (Paris, 1962), lines 52–58.

6. *Les Confessions de saint Augustin dans la tradition littéraire: Antécédents et posterité* (Paris, 1963).

7. See *De Magistro* 1.1, on *commemoratio* and the remarks of Goulven Madec, Bibliothèque Augustinienne 6 (Paris, 1976), 536–38.

8. For a contemporary statement in defense of this view, see John Searle, in the Introduction to "Consciousness, Explanatory Inversion, and Cognitive Science," *Behavioral and Brain Sciences* 13 (1990): 585–96.

9. One of the best known of these popularizations is Colin Morris, *The Discovery of the Individual, 1050–1200* (London, 1972).

10. Internal forces have in particular received considerable attention since the time of the pioneering studies of Dom O. Lottin. For a useful dossier of research materials, see Pierre Courcelle, *Connais-tu toi-même de Socrate à saint Bernard*, vol. 1 (Paris, 1974), vols. 2–3 (Paris, 1975); for an interesting discussion of the hermeneutics in these materials, see Karl F. Morrison, *The Mimetic Tradition of Reform in the West* (Princeton, N.J., 1982) and *"I am You": The Hermeneutics of Empathy in Western Literature, Theology, and Art* (Princeton, N.J., 1988).

11. Two important studies in this field are Mary Carruthers, *The Book of Memory: A Study of Memory in Medieval Culture* (Cambridge, 1990) and Janet Coleman, *Ancient and Medieval Memories: Studies in the Reconstruction of the Past* (Cambridge, 1992). Carruthers has recently supplemented her earlier research in *The Craft of Thought: Meditation, Rhetoric, and the Making of Images, 400–1200* (Cambridge, 1998).

12. Two studies in this field are Michael M. Clanchy, *From Memory to Written Record: England, 1066–1307* (London, 1979), and Brian Stock, *The Implications of Literacy: Written Language and Models of Interpretation in the Eleventh and Twelfth Centuries* (Princeton, N.J., 1983).

13. "Consciousness of Self and Perceptions of Individuality," in *Renaissance and Renewal in the Twelfth Century*, ed. Robert L. Benson and Giles Constable (Cambridge, Mass., 1982), 263–95.

14. In this paragraph I draw on Hazel Rose Markus and Shinobu Kitayama, "Culture and the Self: Implications for Cognition, Emotion, and Motivation," *Psychological Review* 98 (1991): 224–53, here 226–29, 225–26.

15. Thereby introducing another major tradition of thinking, i.e., the linking of the self, linguistic philosophy, and ethics; for a recent restatement of this approach, see Charles Taylor, *Sources of the Self: The Making of Modern Identity* (Cambridge, Mass., 1989), esp. 3–107. It is important however to stress that there were different conceptions of the relationship between intentions and personal narratives after the eleventh century. For Anselm, the context of intentions is a narrative that is already written, as it is for Augustine. By contrast, Abelard sees the context of intentions as a narrative that we write and enact for ourselves, whence his emphasis on assent.

16. The most recent review of the evidence is Constant J. Mews, *The Lost Love Letters of Heloise and Abelard: Perceptions of Dialogue in Twelfth-Century France* (New York, 1999).

17. See Seth Lerer, " 'Transgressio Studii': Writing and Sexuality in Guibert of Nogent," *Stanford French Review* 14 (1990): 243–66, and Sarah Spence, *Texts and the Self in the Twelfth Century* (Cambridge, 1996), 55–83.

18. E.g., in vision; see *De Rebus a Se Gestis*, c. 12, ed. J. S. Brewer, *Giraldi Cambrensis Opera*, vol. 1 (London, 1861), 64.

19. Two important studies of this phenomenon are Jeremy Worthen, "The Self in the Text: Guigo I the Carthusian, William of St. Thierry and Hugh of St. Victor," dissertation, Toronto, 1992 and Spence, *Texts and the Self in the Twelfth Century*.

20. *Hugues de Saint-Victor: Six Opuscules Spirituels*, ed. Roger Baron, Sources chrétiennes 155 (Paris, 1969), 44–59, to which reference is made by chapter and line.

21. A notion summed up around 1100 by William Firmat: "Otium sine litteris mors est et vivi hominis sepultura"; *In amorem clausti et desiderium lectionis divini*, ed. G. Morin, *Revue bénédictine* 31 (1914–19): 248.

22. As Adam of Dryburgh put it, "Sermo quippe sacrae lectionis animae refectio est"; *Sermo* 9.12, *Patrologia Latina* 198.530A.

23. A hagiographic genre whose features are illuminated in Aviad M. Kleinberg, *Prophets in Their Own Country: Living Saints and the Making of Sainthood in the Later Middle Ages* (Chicago, 1992).

24. On this issue, see Dyan Elliott, *Spiritual Marriage: Sexual Abstinence in Medieval Wedlock* (Princeton, N.J.,1993), 208–10.

25. *De Meditatione*, 2.1, p. 46, 16–20: "In lectione autem sic considerandum. Primo lectio ad cognoscendam veritatem materiam ministrat, meditatio coaptat, oratio sublevat, operatio componit, contemplatio in ipsa exultat."

Chapter 5. Petrarch's Portrait of Augustine

1. No attempt is made in this essay to summarize the now considerable literature on other aspects of Petrarch's relationship to Renaissance thought. For a recent review, see Kenneth Gouwens, "Perceiving the Past: Renaissance Humanism After the 'Cognitive Turn'," *American Historical Review* 103 (1998): 64–66, 68–69, 76–77. Two recent reviews of Petrarch scholarship are Marco Ariani, *Petrarca* (Rome, 1999), and Vinicio Pacca, *Petrarca* (Bari, 1998). Francisco Rico has contributed important résumé of the place of the *Secretum* in Italian literature in *Letterature italiane: Le Opere*, vol. 1, *Dalle Origini al Cinquecento*, ed. Alberto Asor Rosa (Turin, 1992), 351–78, with a useful bibliographical note, 376–78.

2. *De Utilitate Credendi* 7.17, ed. Goulven Madec, Bibliothèque Augustinienne 8 (Paris, 1982), 246.

3. René Descartes, *Discours de la méthode*, ed. Étienne Gilson, 5th ed. (Paris, 1976), 4.

4. Quoted from the edition of Enrico Carrara in Francesco Petrarca, *Prose*, ed. Guido Martellotti, Pierre Giorgio Ricci, Enrico Carrara, and Enrico Bianchi (Milan, 1955). The translations are mine. An extensive commentary on this text is provided by Francisco Rico, *Vida u Obra de Petrarca*, vol. 1, *Lectura del "Secretum"* (Chapel Hill, N.C.,1974).

5. The contributions to the complex question of the dating of the *Secretum* are briefly summarized by Pacca, *Petrarca*, 123–24.

6. For the manuscript details, see Rico, *Vida u Obra*, 9–10.

7. Boethius, *Consolatio Philosophiae*, ed. G. Weinberger, *Corpus Scriptorum Ecclesiasticorum Latinorum* 67 (Vienna, 1934), 2: "Haec dum mecum tacitus ipse reputarem querimoniamque lacrimabilem stili officio signarem."

8. Quotations from Seneca are from *Epistulae Morales ad Lucilium*, ed. L. D. Reynolds, 2 vols. (Oxford, 1966); hereafter cited in text by letter and section number.

9. *Aeneid* 1.328.

10. One should not make the assumption that there is a single, "Petrarch" in the work, since the writing of the *Secretum* took place in several phases. Petrarch was thinking about the material in the *Secretum* as early as 1342–43. By 1358, when he completed his final rereading of the dialogue, he may have been in debate with his own earlier reflections.

11. *Scritti Petrarcheschi* (Padua, 1983), 488.

12. Quotations in this paragraph are taken from Petrarch, *Secretum*, 24.

13. Idem, "virum iuxta grandevum ac multa maiestate venerandum." The difference between the historical Augustine and Petrarch's Augustinus has been studied from a number of viewpoints; see, in general, Rico, *Vida u Obra*, 53–55, 68–70 and Hans Baron, *Petrarch's "Secretum": Its Making and Its Meaning* (Cambridge, Mass., 1985), 33–46.

14. Idem, "religiosus aspectus, frons modesta, graves oculi, sobrius incessus."

15. Idem, "circumspiciensque an quisquam secum afforet, an prorsus incomitata mee solitudinis penetrasset."

16. See Victoria Kahn, "The Figure of the Reader in Petrarch's *Secretum*," *Publications of the Modern Language Association* (1985): 154–66.

17. See Pierre Courcelle, "Pétrarque entre Saint Augustin et les Augustins du XIV siècle," *Studi Petrarcheschi* 7 (1961): 7–8, and "Pétrarque lecteur des Confessions," *Rivista di cultura classica e medioevale* 1 (1959): 8–11. On the numerous echoes of the *Confessions* in Petrarch's letters, see Evelyne Luciani, *Les Confessions de saint Augustin dans les lettres de Pétrarque* (Paris, 1982).

18. By holding the *Confessions* in his hand but not reading it, Petrarch would seem to adhere to the medieval notion of the book as a symbol, whereas for Augustine in *Confessions* 8.12, the text of Romans 13: 13–14 is transformative through the act of reading.

19. Cf. Paul Oskar Kristeller, *Eight Philosophers of the Renaissance* (Stanford, Calif., 1964), 14, who notes that Petrarch "transformed the monastic ideal into a secular and literary one."

20. *Secretum*, 26: "aduersus secularum nostri mores."

21. Idem, "sed ut dulcedinem, quam semel ex collocutione percepi, quotiens libuent ex lectione percipiam."

22. Idem, "Tuque ideo, libelle, conventus hominum fugiens, mecum mansisse contentus eris."

23. *Life of Petrarch* (Chicago, 1961), 37; see also Pierre de Nolhac, *Pétrarque et l'humanisme d'après un essai de restitution de sa bibliothèque* (Paris, 1892), 28. Early studies are given by Courcelle, "Pétrarque entre Saint Augustin," 53, n. 8 and "Pétrarque lecteur," 2.

24. Padua, Biblioteca Universitaria, MS 1490, ff. 23r–58r. The glosses have been edited by Francisco Rico, "Petrarca y el *De uera religione*," *Italia medioevale e umanistica* 17 (1974): 313–74.

25. None of these themes are prominent in Augustine's writings down to 401. Petrarch is attracted to Augustine's *Confessions* as an authoritative narrative but less interested in following the evolution of Augustine's thinking between the early writings and the autobiography.

26. Allusions and references to *De Civitate Dei*, along with the single mention of the *Retractationes*, are found in the index to Rico, "Petrarca y el *De uera religione*."

27. See Pierre Courcelle, "Pétrarque lecteur," 4, and, for a recent discussion, my study, *Augustine the Reader: Meditation, Self-Knowledge, and the Ethics of Interpretation* (Cambridge, Mass., 1996), 37–42. On the manuscript evidence, see Giuseppe Billanovich, "Petrarca e Cicerone," *Miscellanea Giovanni Mercati*, vol. 4 (Vatican City, 1946), 88–106.

28. Nor, for that matter, of Laura's equivalent in the *Confessions*, the lover who bore Augustine his son Adeodatus and was subsequently dismissed.

29. On this theme see Marco Santagata, *I frammenti dell'anima: Storia e racconto nel Canzoniere di Petrarca* (Bologna, 1992); also Thomas M. Greene, "Petrarch: The Ontology of the Self," in *The Light in Troy: Imitation and Discovery in Renaissance Poetry* (New Haven, Conn., 1982), 104–26. A historical study of similar issues is Charles Trinkaus, *The Poet as Philosopher: Petrarch and the Formation of Renaissance Consciousness* (New Haven, Conn., 1979).

30. *Secretum*, p. 42: "Ex quo fit, quotiens *Confessionum* tuarum libros lego,

inter duos contrarios affectus, spem videlicet et metum, letis non sine lacrimis interdum legere me arbitrer non alienam sed propriam mee peregrinationis historiam."

31. The image was less likely to occur to authors in earlier medieval centuries owing to the scarcity of books.

32. The relevant texts are assembled by Pacca, *Petrarca,* 34–36, 92–97.

33. His personal situation can be compared to that of Scipio, around whom he builds the plot of *Africa.* Scipio is a lonely hero, but he is never alone.

34. Seneca, *Ep.* 65.21: "Maior sum et ad maiora genitus, quam ut mancipium sim mei corporis."

35. *Secretum,* 146: "Forma quidem tibi visa est tam blanda, tam dulcis, ut in te omnem ex nativis virtutum seminibus preventuram segetem ardentissimi desiderii estibus et assiduo lacrimarum imbre vastaverit." Note the reuse of *dulcis:* earlier, it describes their conversations, later, Petrarch's literary efforts.

36. Idem, "Ista quoque, quam tam predicas ducem a multis te obscenis abstrahens in splendidum impulit baratrum."

37. See the outstanding study of Giles Constable, "Petrarch and Monasticism," in *Francesco Petrarca: Citizen of the World* (Padua and Albany, N.Y., 1980), 58.

38. The bibliography of Petrarch's relationship to monasticism is briefly reviewed by Jean Leclercq, "Temi monastici nell'opera del Petrarca," *Lettere italiane* 43 (1991): 42–44. A fundamental assessment is Constable, "Petrarch and Monasticism," in *Francesco Petrarca,* 53–99. The reception of Petrarch's writings on the religious life by other humanist authors interested in monasticism is reviewed by Anna Maria Voci, *Petrarca e la vita religiosa: Il mito umanistica della vita eremetica* (Rome, 1983), 113–56.

39. Cf. Leclercq, "Temi," 47, 50, 53.

40. See Voci, *Il mito,* 57–81.

Chapter 6. Two Versions of Utopia

1. Thomas Stapleton, *The Life and Illustrious Martyrdom of Sir Thomas More . . . ,* trans. Philip E. Hallett (London, 1928), 9.

2. Nicholas Harpsfield, *The Life and Death of St. Thomas Moore . . . ,* ed. E. V. Hitchcock, intro. R. W. Chambers (London, 1932), 13–14.

3. *Utopia,* ed. Edward Surtz and J. H. Hexter, *The Complete Works of St. Thomas More,* vol. 4 (New Haven, Conn., 1965), 20:

Vtopia priscis dicta, ob infrequentiam,
Nunc ciuitatis aemula Platonicae,
Fortasse uictrix, nam quod illa literis
Delineauit, hoc ego una praestiti,
Viris & opibus, optimisque legibus:
Eutopia merito sum uocanda nomine.

More was an accomplished epigrammist; on his style see Susan L. Holahan, "More's Epigrams on Henry Abyngdon," *Moreana* 3 (1968): 21–26.

4. For an argument against More's interpretation of Plato's *Republic* as an abstract society, see Kevin Corrigan, "The Function of the Ideal in Plato's *Republic* and in St. Thomas More's *Utopia*," *Moreana* 27 (1990): 27–49.

5. Studies of Augustine's influence on More include R. C. Marius, "Thomas More and the Early Church Fathers," *Traditio* 24 (1968): 382–84, 401–2; H. Meulon, "More homme d'action: Le défenseur de la cité," *Moreana* 6 (1969): 89–90; Leland Miles, "Patristic Comforters on More's *Dialogue of Comfort*," *Moreana* 8 (1971): 10–11; Louis L. Martz, "More as Author: The Virtues of Digression," *Moreana* 16 (1979): 109–10; and, on John Colet, whose use of patristic sources may have influenced More, Robert Peters, "John Colet's Knowledge and Use of Patristics," *Moreana* 6 (1969): 48, 50–51. The best general guide is found in the notes to *The Complete Works of St. Thomas More*, vol. 12, ed. Louis L. Martz and Frank Manley (New Haven, Conn., 1976). In judging More's debts to Augustine, consideration has to be given to the possibility that these may be based on medieval interpretations, such as those found in the theology of the Charterhouse, since it was some years after his lectures that Vives's edition of *De Civitate Dei* appeared. On the possibility that the "socialism" of More and Vives was influenced by their interpretation of Augustine, see Alain Guy, "Vives socialiste et *L'Utopie* de More," *Moreana* 8 (1971): 263–80.

6. Books 1 to 10 of *De Civitate Dei* attempt to refute polytheism, while book 11 begins the biblical history of the two cities. In this second segment, books 11 to 14 discuss the origins of the opposition between the earthly and the heavenly city; books 15 to 22 treat the evolution of the relationship in a theological context.

7. *De Civitate Dei*, 11.1, *Corpus Christianorum Series Latina* 48, 321–22: "Nunc . . . de duarum ciuitatum, terrenae scilicet et caelestis, quas in hoc interim saeculo perplexas quodam modo diximus inuicemque permixtas, exortu . . . disputare . . . adgrediar."

8. Ibid., 11.2, p. 322 (with some explanatory words added in my paraphrase): "Magnum est admodum rarum uniuersam creaturam corpoream et incorpoream consideratam compertamque mutabilem intentione mentis excedere atque incommutabilem Dei substantiam peruenire et illic discere ex ipso, quod cunctam naturam, quae non est quod ipse, non fecit nisi ipse."

9. Augustine, *Confessiones* 11.27.35–36.

10. The most elaborate discussion of this issue in Augustine's thought is found in *De Trinitate*, 15.10.17 ff., *Corpus Christianorum Series Latina* 50, 483 ff.; for a discussion of the relationship to the *Confessions*, see my *Augustine the Reader: Meditation, Self-Knowledge, and the Ethics of Interpretation* (Cambridge, Mass., 1996), 243–48.

11. This may be the earliest argument for monotheism based on a philosophy of language.

12. *De Civitate Dei* 11.2, 322, lines 6–12.

13. The earliest form of the argument is in *Soliloquia*, 2.1, which is discussed in Chapter 3.

14. Edmund Husserl, *Cartesian Meditations: An Introduction to Phenomenology*, trans. Dorian Cairns (The Hague, 1973): 27–29.

15. *De Civitate Dei* 11.2.30–31: "Per hoc enim mediator, per hoc quod homo, per hoc et uia."

16. *Conf.*, 7.10; cf. Plotinus, *Enn.*, 1.8.13, and ultimately, Plato, *Pol.*, 273d; on the subsequent usage, see above all Pierre Courcelle, "Tradition néo-platonicienne et traditions chrétiennes de la "région de dissemblance (Platon, *Politique* 273 d)," *Archives d'histoire doctrinale et littéraire du moyen âge*, Année 1957 (1958): 5–33. The historical origins of the notion of alienation are outlined by R. A. Markus, " 'Alienatio': Philosophy and Eschatology in the Development of an Augustinian Idea," *Studia Patristica* 9, 3 (Berlin, 1966): 431–50.

17. A view shared by pagan and Christian thinkers in late antiquity; see Pierre Hadot, *Qu'est-ce que la philosophie antique?* (Paris, 1995): 235–37.

18. *De Civitate Dei* 11.3, 323, lines 15–16: "ita de his, quae animo ac mente sentiuntur."

19. Ibid., 11.2, 322.

20. On More's possible etymological route through Ficino's translation of Plato's *Politics*, see Paul A. Sawada, "Toward the Definition of Utopia," *Moreana* 8 (1971): 139.

21. On More's satirical intention, see C. S. Lewis, *English Literature in the Sixteenth Century Excluding Drama* (Oxford, 1954), 167–70.

22. *Thomas More* (London, 1935).

23. Ibid.,119.

24. Other aspects of More's potential debt to the Middle Ages are examined by P. Albert Duhamel, "Medievalism of More's *Utopia*," *Studies in Philology* 52 (1955): 99–126. The literature is reviewed by J. H. Hexter in the Introduction to *Utopia* (1965), xlv–liv.

25. For an authoritative review of the issues, see J. H. Hexter, *More's "Utopia": The Biography of an Idea* (Princeton, N.J., 1952) and his introduction to *Utopia*, cxii–cxxiii. For an intelligent criticism within a warm reception of Hexter's approach, see the review of the Yale edition of *Utopia* by Douglas Bush, *Moreana* 6 (1969): 89–90.

26. More seems to have anticipated the norm adopted by the European Community of a work week of 35 hours.

27. See John J. Schaeffer, "Socratic Method in More's *Utopia*," *Moreana* 18 (1981): 5–20. On the Renaissance use of the literary form of the dialogue, see in general David Marsh, *The Quattrocento Dialogue: Classical Tradition and Humanist Innovation* (Cambridge, Mass., 1980).

28. For thoughtful remarks on this transformation, see Seth Lerer, *Boethius and Dialogue: Literary Method in "The Consolation of Philosophy"* (Princeton, N.J.,1985), 14–93.

29. On the history of this type of conversation, see the brilliant *esquisse* of Marc Fumaroli, *Le genre des genres littéraires français: La conversation*, The Zaharoff Lecture for 1990–91 (Oxford, 1992), 6–10.

30. Or *Philebus*; on this possibility, see Judith Jones, "The *Philebus* and the Philosophy of Pleasure in Thomas More's *Utopia*," *Moreana* 8 (1971): 61–70.

31. A point made by Enrico Quattrochi, "Injustice, Not Counselling: The

Theme of Book One of *Utopia*," *Moreana* 8 (1971): 20. On the problem of reform see Robbin S. Johnson, "The Argument for Reform in More's *Utopia*," *Moreana* 8 (1971): 123–34, especially the excellent summary, p. 130.

32. *Sermo* 81.8, *Patrologia Latina* 38.504.

33. *Augustine of Hippo* (London, 1967), 305.

34. For a brilliant analysis of More's career along these lines, see the enduring essay of Stephen Greenblatt in *Renaissance Self-Fashioning: From More to Shakespeare* (Chicago, 1980), 11–73.

Chapter 7. *Lectio Spiritualis*

1. *Literary Language and Its Public in Late Latin Antiquity and in the Middle Ages*, trans. Ralph Manheim (London, 1965), 6.

2. Quotations in the following discussion are from *Soliloquiorum Libri Duo*, 1.1, ed. Wolfgang Hörmann, *Corpus Scriptorum Ecclesiasticorum Latinorum* 89 (Vienna, 1986), 3–4.

3. Ibid., 1.1, p. 3: "Nec ista dictari debent; nam solitudinem meram desiderant."

4. Ibid.: "Deinde quod invenis paucis conclusiunculis breviter conlige."

5. For a review of these practices, see Pierre Hadot, *Qu'est-ce que la philosophie antique?* (Paris, 1995),145–264.

6. There are of course precedents for the philosophical monologue, among them Epictetus, *Discourses* 1.17.3, which anticipates *Sol.*, 1.1 in speaking of reason, which engages in the analysis of itself; cf. Epictetus 1.20.1ff., on self-contemplation.

7. For an introduction to this subject, see "*Lectio divina* et lecture spirituelle," *Dictionnaire de Spiritualité*, vol. 9 (Paris, 1976), cols. 470–510.

8. Dom Jean Leclercq, *L'Amour des lettres et le désir de Dieu: Initiation aux auteurs monastiques du Moyen Age* (Paris, 1957).

9. *Ep.*, 1.15, *Patrologia Latina* 4.226B.

10. E.g., *Scala Claustralium sive Tractatus de Modo Orandi*, cc. 1–2, *Patrologia Latina* 184, 475–77.

11. Jerome, *Ep. ad Marcellam*, 43.2, *Patrologia Latina* 22.478C.

12. *Vita Antonii* 55, *Patrologia Graeca* 26.845A.

13. *Reg. ben.*, c. 48.

14. J. Alvarez de Paz, *De Exterminatione Mali et Promotione Boni libri quinque* (Lyons, 1613), book 3, part 5, section 2, chapter 2: *De lectione spiritualis*, 964a: "Spiritualem autem lectionem vocamus, qua mysticos libros et spirituales tractatus euoluimus, in quibus non solam rerum spiritualium notitiam, sed multos magis earum gustum et affectum quaerimus." This text, which merits an extensive study, links the practices of *lectio divina* and *lectio spiritualis* in a single devotional program through the Fathers and Bonaventure.

15. *Inst.*, 5.14; 11.3 and 6; 12.11–14.

16. *De Libris Legendis a Monacho*, ed. Louis-Ellier du Pin, vol. 2 (Anvers, 1706), 709B.

17. *De Considerationibus quas Debet Habere Princeps, Opera*, vol. 3, col. 233.

18. *Space Between Words: The Origins of Silent Reading,* (Stanford, Calif., 1997).

19. For a review of positions, see Aimé Solignac, "Image et ressemblance II: Pères de l'Église," *Dictionnaire de Spiritualité,* vol. 7, cols. 1406–25.

20. Quotations from this section are from the edition of the *Secretum* by Enrico Carrara in Francesco Petrarca, *Prose,* ed. Guido Martellotti, Pierre Giorgio Ricci, Enrico Carrara, and Enrico Bianchi (Milan, 1955), 121–22.

21. Ibid., 122: "Imo vero inter legendo plurimum; libro autem e manibus elapso assensio simul omnis intercidit."

Index

Abelard, Peter, 5, 24, 25–26, 55, 60–61, 63
Alan of Lille, 17, 39, 60, 70, 110
Ambrose of Milan, 2, 16, 46, 48, 79, 89
Ammianus Marcellinus, 41
Ammonius, 39, 42, 48
Anselm of Canterbury, 5, 27, 32, 63, 104
Anselm of Laon, 61
Anthony, St., 18, 44, 69, 80, 106
Apuleius, 41
Aquinas, St. Thomas, 27, 99, 114
Aristotle, 5, 24, 33, 68, 99
Ascoli, Graziado Isaia, 101
Auerbach, Erich, 38–51, 102
Augustine of Hippo, 1–8, 10, 15–17, 20, 24–37, 39, 41, 55–58, 64–66, 69–94, 97, 101–5, 110

Bede, the Venerable, 15
Bellerophon, 81–82
Benedict, St., 16, 105, 106, 109
Benton, John F., 59
Berengar of Tours, 1
Bernard of Clairvaux, 17, 67, 84, 108–9
Bernard Silvestris, 70, 110
Boethius, 5, 17, 24, 74–75, 104
Bonaventure, St., 108, 112
Bonnefoy, Yves, 9
Brentano, Franz, 27
Brown, Peter, 99
Bruner, Jerome, 27
Burckhardt, Jacob, 8
Butler, Samuel, 86

Cardano, Girolamo, 9
Carterius, 40–41, 50
Cassian, John, 105, 107
Cellini, Benvenuto, 9
Chambers, R. W., 95, 100
Christina of Markyate, 65–66
Christine de Pizan, 9, 26

Christ, 18, 20, 60, 93
Cicero, 13, 19, 24, 39, 75, 78, 81–82, 87, 98, 103, 109, 112–13
Courcelle, Pierre, 11, 57
Crashaw, Richard, 22
Croce, Benedetto, 102
Curtius, Ernst Robert, 25, 102, 113

Dante Alighieri, 17, 25–26, 39, 49, 68, 75, 95, 102, 104, 110, 114
David of Augsburg, 106–7
Descartes, René, 12–13, 15, 20, 25–26, 56, 68, 72–73
Diez, Friedrich, 101
Dilthey, Wilhelm, 9
Diogenes Laertius, 46
Dionigi da Borgo San Sepolcro, 85, 113
Dionysius, the Pseudo-Areopagite, 60, 112
Donne, John, 22

Epictetus, 3, 31, 55
Epicurus, 15, 32
Erasmus, Desiderius, 13, 39, 65, 77, 110, 114
Eriugena, Johannes Scottus, 39, 60, 112
Evagrius Ponticus, 19, 105

Francis of Assisi, 19, 67–69, 80
Freud, Sigmund, 49

Gerson, Jean, 108
Gilles, Peter, 98
Giraldus Cambrensis, 62
Greene, Graham, 34
Gregory of Nyssa, 111
Gregory of Tours, 41, 50
Gregory the Great, 14–16, 38, 105, 108
Gröber, Gustav, 102
Groote, Gerard, 110

Guibert of Nogent, 61–63, 110
Guigo I, 63–64, 65, 80

Hadot, Pierre, 14
Harpsfield, Nicolas, 87
Heidegger, Martin, 9
Héloïse, 55, 60–61, 65
Herbert, George, 22
Herder, Johann Gottfried, 9
Homer, 81
Horace, 39, 78
Hugh of St. Victor, 1, 17, 63–66, 70
Humbert of Romans, 106–7
Humboldt, Wilhelm von, 101–2
Husserl, Edmund, 9, 27, 106
Huxley, Aldous, 86

Ignatius of Loyola, 22, 108

Jean de Fécamp, 63
Jerome, St., 38, 106
John, St., gospel of, 46
John of the Cross, 112
Judaism, 35, 36, 60, 73, 105, 111
Julian of Norwich, 19

Kempe, Marjorie, 9
Klemperer, Victor, 102

Lanfranc of Bec, 1
Leclercq, Jean, 15, 105
Locke, John, 26
Luther, Martin, Lutherans, 76, 96

Macrobius, 98
Manichaeism, 2, 4, 45, 79
Marcus Aurelius, 3, 10, 19, 24, 32,
    51–56, 64, 86
Marius Victorinus, 39
Martellotti, Guido, 76
Maximus the Confessor, 60, 112
Misch, Georg, 9
Mombaer, Jean, 108
Monica, 79, 91
Montaigne, Michel de, 7, 13, 68, 76, 84,
    109, 114
More, Thomas, 6, 19, 65

Nebridius, 31, 45
Nicholas of Cusa, 73
Nietzsche, Friedrich, 9
Norden, Eduard, 38–39

Origen, 105–6

Orwell, George, 86
Othloh of St. Emmeram, 80, 110

Paris, Gaston, 101
Pascal, Blaise, 7, 13, 25, 114
Paul, St., 22, 28, 34, 46, 58–59, 77, 79,
    98, 105
Paulinus of Nola, 44
Pelagianism, 32–33
Petrarca, Francesco, 5, 9, 11, 13, 17, 22,
    25, 68– 69, 71–85, 102, 104, 109
Philo of Alexandria, 15, 24
Plato, 3, 6, 24, 32, 33, 53, 72, 74, 86–100
Plotinus, 2–3, 10, 22, 24, 28, 33, 39–51,
    55, 58, 69, 79, 86–87, 92, 98, 103
Polemo, 46
Porphyry, 18, 28, 39–51, 79
Proust, Marcel, 23
Prudentius, 17, 39

Quintilian, 24–25

Raynouard, François, 101
Rogatianus, 48, 49
Roper, William, 87

Saenger, Paul, 108
Seneca, 3, 10, 13, 19, 24, 31, 51–56, 74,
    78, 81, 83–84, 86, 103, 109, 112–13
Socrates, 3, 25, 97, 104, 113
Southey, Richard, 8
Spitzer, Leo, 102
Stapleton, Thomas, 87
Stein, Gertrude, 27

Tacitus, 38, 41, 50
Thomas à Kempis, 19, 110

Valerius Maximus, 85
Vico, Giovanni Battista, 7
Vossler, Karl, 102
Virgil, 3, 74–75, 78

Warburg, Aby, 102
Weber, Max, 8–9, 59, 66–67, 96
Wilkins, Ernest Hatch, 78
William of St. Thierry, 85, 104, 106
Wilmart, André, 16
Wittgenstein, Ludwig, 33
Wittinton, Robert, 100

Xenocrates, 46

Acknowledgments

I would like to acknowledge the support that I have received from the Collège de France, the Fondazione Giorgio Cini in Venice, and the Accademia Nazionale dei Lincei in Rome.

Among numerous individuals to whom I owe personal debts of gratitude are Yves Bonnefoy, Vittore Branca, Peter Brown, Ralph Cohen, Giles Constable, Pierre and Ilsetraut Hadot, Maruja Jackman, Carlo Ossola, Javier Teixidor, and Andreas and Vanna Wittenburg. I have been encouraged by a number of junior colleagues of exceptional talent, among them Linda Bisello, Dario Brancato, Stefano Cracolici, and Sabrina Stroppa. Two librarians have rendered invaluable service: Claudine Croyère at Études Augustiniennes, Paris, and Caroline Suma at the Pontifical Institute of Mediaeval Studies, Toronto.

Earlier versions of some of the material appeared in the following lectures and publications, reprinted by permission.

"Ethical Values and the Literary Imagination in the Later Ancient World," *New Literary History* 29 (1998): 1–13.

"The Self and Literary Experience in Late Antiquity and the Middle Ages," *New Literary History* 25 (1994): 839–52.

"Reading, Writing, and the Self: Petrarch and His Forerunners," *New Literary History* 26 (1995): 717–30. Used with the kind permission of Ralph Cohen, editor of *New Literary History*.

"La connaissance de soi au Moyen Age," Leçon Inaugurale, Chaire Internationale, Collège de France, Paris, 1998. Copyright Collège de France, 1998.

"Literary Realism in the Later Ancient Period," *Literary History and the Challenge of Philology: The Legacy of Erich Auerbach,* ed. Seth Lerer (Stanford, Calif.), 1996, pp. 143–55. Copyright © 1996 Board of Trustees of the Leland Stanford Junior University. By permission of Stanford University Press.

"Città Eterne: Agostino e Tomasso More," Inaugural Lecture, XLI Corso di Alta Cultura, Fondazione Giorgio Cini, Venice, 1999. An English version was delivered as the Gryphon Lecture, Rare Book Library, University of Toronto, March 2000.

"*Lectio divina* e *Lectio spiritualis*: La scrittura come pratica contemplativa nel Medioevo," Inaugural Lecture, Convegno Internazionale, La cultura letteraria italiana e l'identità europea, Accademia Nazionale dei Lincei, Rome, 6–8 April 2000. The Italian version of this essay revised by Dario Brancato appeared in *Lettere italiane* 2 (2000): 169–83.